Ominous clouds _____ r in Timisoara, Romania, in _____ years of
harassment for spe _____ nunists,
Pastor Laszlo Tokes v _____ church. But he
refused to abandon ___ congregation. They had always
stood with him, even after a member of his church council
had been slain outside the city the previous September.
Nothing – not even numerous death threats to him and
his family – could deter Laszlo. In November 1989, four
masked men broke into his home and attacked him and his
family with axes. A crowd of loyal supporters gathered
outside Laszlo's church in December. The police arrived,
arrested Laszlo, and dragged him and his pregnant wife
away. Having fallen into the hands of the Communists,
Laszlo Tokes was presumed dead.

As the crowds in Timisoara swelled to 50,000 and then to
100,000, the secret police were helpless. The tempest raged
on and soon spread to the capital, Bucharest. In just a
matter of days, the Communist regime was overthrown
and its tyrant dictator executed.

In the Eye of the Romanian Storm tells the dramatic, un-
forgettable story of the personal faith and courage of Pastor
Laszlo Tokes, hero and catalyst of the Romanian Revolution. This compelling biography presents a firsthand look
at history in the making during the final days of the
Ceausescan regime. Your heart will go out to Pastor Laszlo
and our persecuted Romanian brothers and sisters. You
will also share in their triumphant release from tyranny
through the tremendous power of faith and gain a new and
deeper appreciation of the precious gift of freedom that we
so often take for granted.

IN THE EYE OF THE ROMANIAN STORM

THE HEROIC STORY OF PASTOR LASZLO TOKES

Felix Corley and John Eibner

Fleming H. Revell Company
Old Tappan, New Jersey

Scripture quotations in this publication are from the Holy Bible, New International Version. Copyright © 1973, 1978, 1984 International Bible Society. Used by permission of Zondervan Bible Publishers.

Translation of Laszlo Tokes's television interview used by permission of Hungarian Human Rights Foundation.

Library of Congress Cataloging-in-Publication Data

Corley, Felix.
    In the eye of the Romanian storm / Felix Corley and John Eibner.
        p.   cm.
    ISBN 0-8007-5379-8
    1. Tokes, Laszlo. 2. Biserica Reformată (Romania)—Bishops—
Biography. 3. Reformed Church—Romania—Timişoara—
Clergy—Biography. 4. Transylvania (Romania)—Ethnic rela-
tions. 5. Communism and Christianity—Romania—History.
6. Persecution—Romania—History—20th century. 7. Timişoara
(Romania)—Politics and government. 8. Timişoara (Romania)—
Church history. 9. Romania—Politics and government—
1944–1989. 10. Romania—Politics and government—1989.
I. Eibner, John. II. Title.
    BX9480.R63T6   1990
    949.803—dc20   90-43205
                                                              CIP

Copyright © 1990 by Felix Corley and John Eibner
Published by the Fleming H. Revell Company
Old Tappan, New Jersey 07675
Printed in the United States of America

This book is dedicated to the memory of
Peter Timothy Corley (1962–1989)
Requiescat in Pace

Contents

Acknowledgments

This book could not have been written without the help of many people. We are grateful to members of the Tokes family, including Istvan, Laszlo, Stephen, Jozsef and Anna.

We conducted interviews with members of Laszlo's congregations in Timisoara and Dej, and eyewitnesses of the Bucharest demonstrations. In Cluj we spoke to a number of people connected with the Reformed Church. At the bishop's office in Oradea we spoke with Deputy Bishop Attila Veres-Kovacs. In Hungary we interviewed— among others—Janos and Irma Molnar, Attila Ara-Kovacs and Miklos Kovacs. The Hungarian Institute in Budapest, the Hungarian Human Rights Foundation (which provided the translation of Laszlo's TV interview), Keston College and Glaube in der Zweiten Welt have provided useful documentation. The filmmakers of Fekete Doboz in Budapest kindly made film available.

The aid organization S.O.S. Transylvania, Agnes Balint, Andras Miko and Nick Marshall were indispensable on the long road to Transylvania.

FC AND JE

Note

Many towns and villages in Romania have three names: a Romanian, Hungarian and German form. We have largely used the Romanian versions. A list of a few of the most frequently mentioned towns is given below:

Romanian	Hungarian	German
Cluj	Kolozsvar	Klausenburg
Timisoara	Temesvar	Temeschburg
Oradea	Nagyvarad	Grosswardein
Sibiu	Nagyszeben	Hermannstadt
Brasov	Brasso	Kronstadt
Tirgu Mures	Marosvasarhely	
Dej	Des	

Chronology

April 1, 1952: Laszlo born in Cluj.

1971–1975: Studied at Theological Institute in Cluj.

1975–1977: Worked as assistant pastor in Brasov and Zernesti.

1977: Transferred to Dej.

1984: Removed by Bishop Nagy as assistant pastor of Dej.

December 15, 1985: Laszlo married Edith Joo in Dej.

July, 1986: Began work in Timisoara parish.

September 6, 1988: Arad Deanery protest against systematization policy.

March 20, 1989: Laszlo attacked the government in filmed interview.

April 1, 1989: Laszlo informed of his suspension as pastor of Timisoara.

July 24, 1989: Hungarian TV broadcast March interview.

November 2, 1989: Masked men broke into Laszlo's flat in an apparent murder attempt.

December 15, 1989: Date set for eviction; demonstrations began around Laszlo's church.

December 17, 1989: Laszlo and Edith dragged from the church and taken to Mineu; protests continued in Timisoara.

December 21, 1989: Ceausescu spoke to rally in Bucharest. Speech interrupted after protests. Riots in capital.

December 22, 1989: Ceausescu and his wife fled. National Salvation Front declared itself in power. Laszlo's interrogators fled.

December 25, 1989: Ceausescus tried and executed.

March 29, 1990: Laszlo elected bishop of Oradea.

May 8, 1990: Installation as bishop.

T = TIMISOARA   TM = TIRGU MURES

O = ORADEA   B = BRASOV

C = CLUJ   S = SIBIU

D = DEJ   M = MINEU

ROMANIA

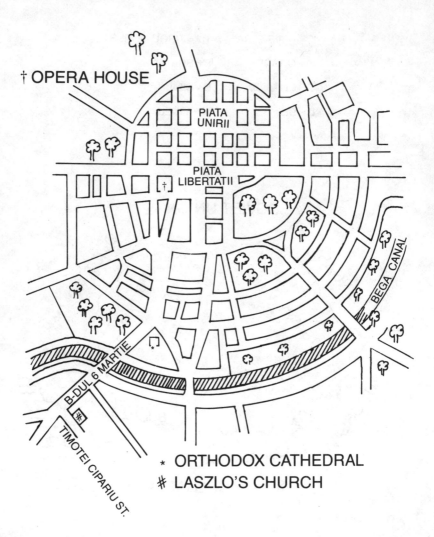

† OPERA HOUSE

PIATA UNIRII

PIATA LIBERTATII

BEGA CANAL

B-DUL 6 MARTIE

TIMOTEI CIPARIU ST.

* ORTHODOX CATHEDRAL
# LASZLO'S CHURCH

TIMISOARA

IN THE EYE OF
THE

**THE HEROIC STORY
OF
PASTOR LASZLO TOKES**

ROMANIAN
STORM

ONE

Romania Explodes

The front gate crashed to the ground. The secret police forced their way into the building of the Reformed Church in Timisoara. It was three in the morning. They came to drag away the courageous young pastor, Laszlo Tokes. Laszlo knew it would be only a few minutes before the intruders would reach his apartment beneath the church, where he waited with his wife Edith and six courageous friends. The eight of them jumped into frenzied action. The pastor quickly donned his clerical gown.

They raced from door to door, hastily locking them as they ran out of the apartment and into the cellar that linked the apartment to the rest of the church complex. Rats scuttled in the darkness as Laszlo helped his pregnant wife through the cellar. Laszlo looked around the door into the yard. It was pitch-black outside. Sporadic gunfire mingled with the distant shouting. Three secret police scrambled over the fence into the courtyard of the church.

Laszlo and Edith climbed up a ladder from the yard to the balcony outside the church, thirty feet up in the darkness. Breathing heavily, they were closely followed by Edith's brother-in-law and a student. The four others stayed behind to divert the attention of the intruders for a few precious moments.

Laszlo and Edith made it into the church. The holiness of God's sanctuary was vividly before them. Laszlo had planned this flight into the sanctuary, his mind full of biblical imagery. The house of God has traditionally been a refuge from persecution. Laszlo half hoped those who had come to arrest him would respect the sanctity of the church. Brutality might be kept to a minimum. Laszlo went to the table of the Lord and opened the Bible. The four prayed in the darkness.

Laszlo's mind raced with jumbled thoughts of his two years' turbulent stay in Timisoara. Now they were here for the last time. He looked up at the pulpit, shrouded in darkness. How many times had he stood there and preached the Good News? He bowed his head in prayer.

The police burst in within seconds—first a few, then wave after wave. Some wore uniforms, others did not. They pounced on Laszlo, ripping his robe. Blood gushed from his nose as the beating continued in the darkened church. Edith was grabbed and hustled down the stairs to Laszlo's office. The bruised and battered pastor was dragged down after his wife. The room was full of police. Then he saw the State Secretary for Religious Affairs, Ion Cumpanasu, from Bucharest and his Timisoara County counterpart Mihai Teperdel.

The State Secretary smiled and offered his hand as if he were meeting Laszlo at a church social. The delirious Laszlo reached out to accept the hand of his persecutor. Then an eviction order was shoved into Laszlo's face. He instinctively hesitated. The thugs immediately leapt on him again. He signed.

Laszlo and Edith were dragged out of the church toward some cars. The darkened vehicles sat by the gate with their engines already running. As Laszlo struggled with the police, he could see his wife being pulled toward one of the cars. She was shrieking. The blood poured from his wounds. Laszlo could do nothing to help his wife. He was powerless as he saw her being bundled into the car. With a heavy blow to the back of her head, the shrieks stopped.

Laszlo was sure the men were about to murder them. He slumped in the back of the car, his head throbbing, feeling faint, exhausted, the echo of his wife's screams ringing in his ears. Would this be their last journey? Laszlo expected the cars to separate and take them to their chosen places of execution. Then he noticed the two cars were sticking together. Hope briefly flickered that they might be heading for the Hungarian border. This would be too good to be true.

Within minutes, the convoy turned into the forecourt of Timisoara's police station. Corpses were strewn everywhere. The guards prevented Laszlo from looking out of the window. The convoy was reorganized and pulled out of the forecourt. The cars drove from Timisoara into the black unknown. Laszlo slumped into fitful, exhausted sleep.

The Brewing Storm

The storm around Laszlo had been brewing for months. The Communist regime hated him for his outspoken views. Like an Old Testament prophet, he condemned injustice in Romanian society and upheld basic human rights. He defended the rights of his own group—the 2-million-strong Hungarian minority in Romania. Laszlo knew that truth is the greatest enemy of dictatorship. The regime had to silence him.

A final eviction decree was issued on December 7. There was no right of appeal: they had to leave the apartment and church by December 15. The Sunday after the court hearing, Laszlo asked his congregation to come peacefully on Friday the 15th to witness the eviction. He doubted many people would come. Fear had gripped the congregation. They had seen one member of the church murdered, another thrown from a streetcar. Many had received death threats. No one dared send their children to church for religious instruction.

Laszlo was surprised early on Friday morning when the housekeeper came running from the window. She shouted that a crowd of 200 supporters had gathered outside the church. Tears filled Laszlo's eyes. He could not believe that, after all the fear and terror, his people were prepared to risk so much for him. The police moved them on, but they kept gathering again. He longed to address them but did not know what to say. Finally he went to the window. Speaking simply, he urged them to disperse peacefully. "My brothers and sisters," he said, "I hope no more will come here on my account. Please go home in peace." But the people shouted up to him: "We will stand by you till night!"

The crowd grew with each passing hour. Laszlo was surprised to see people who never came near the church. They saw the broken windows and became indignant. The crowd tried to bring the besieged family some food. Laszlo's wife—who was three months pregnant—had no milk. As policemen barred the way to those bringing food, the crowd grew angrier. Officials from the British and American embassies in far-off Bucharest arrived. This was the last thing the government wanted: the Romanian authorities were used to dealing with their dissidents without the glare of international publicity.

The police persisted in trying to remove the crowd. The people grew more resolved. Finally the ever-growing crowds shoved the police away. Well-wishers passed loaves of bread through the windows. Milk, potatoes, eggs and meat followed. In a country of severe food shortages, the Tokeses' front room now looked like a foreign food store. Laszlo was overwhelmed and tried to turn some of the produce away. But his supporters pressed it on him.

More and more people arrived as the elders phoned around to members of Laszlo's Hungarian congregation. They were soon joined by ethnic Romanians. By mid-afternoon of that Friday, Romanians were in a majority. When Laszlo again addressed the people, he spoke in Romanian.

Laszlo was touched by this support. Relations between Romanians and the Hungarian minority had often been bitter. But now they had a common enemy: the malevolent forces of Nicolae Ceausescu's dictatorial regime. Laszlo was encouraged by the unprecedented support. But he felt a sense of foreboding all day. Deep down he knew that the long-postponed blow was about to fall.

As the government's sentries on Laszlo's house melted away into the crowd, people rushed in through the gate. They poured up the stairs and into Laszlo's flat, offering their support and best wishes. They brought gifts, which they left in the apartment or on the altar in the church upstairs. The people were preparing for Christmas. For Laszlo, it was hard to think of the forthcoming festival. What would he preach to his people about?

The building was like the nerve center of a sudden revolution, Laszlo thought. People came and went in freedom. The mood was suddenly carefree. But Laszlo could not shake off the feeling of impending doom. Here and there he recognized Securitate agents in the crowd. From a high building across the narrow street, the secret police were filming everything that was going on. Laszlo was preparing for a siege.

The mayor of Timisoara, Petru Mots, arrived at the head of a delegation late on Friday evening. The group came through the hostile crowd in the dark. There was no lighting in the street. Mots ordered the many broken windows in the apartment to be mended and for the garbage, which had not been collected for a week, to be taken away. He promised everything. But the crowd refused to believe him. When he started to speak, they booed and hissed, drowning his words. Without Laszlo's calming influence, the seething crowd would have lynched Mots.

Laszlo went out to the gate at 10:00 P.M. to speak to him. The mayor again promised everything would be all right. Laszlo would be allowed to remain in the church. They would give him official permission to live in Timisoara. All Laszlo had to do was send the crowds away.

The mayor took down the names of those the crowd had chosen to form a negotiating team.

When the window repair team arrived, the people would not let them through, fearing a trick. It seemed odd that it would take five men to mend a few windows. One of the men was dressed in traditional Securitate garb—a leather coat. Finally the crowd let them through. One man repaired the windows while the others watched.

The people did not believe Mots's promises. All night long they maintained a candlelight vigil below Laszlo's window. The exhausted pastor and his wife tried to sleep. Laszlo was astonished to find them still there as he woke up in the morning. By now the whole town knew of the drama that was being played out around him.

The mayor turned up again. He had brought along a team of doctors to examine Laszlo's wife in an attempt to curry favor. For the past week Edith had suffered a serious ear infection. Three times her doctor had been turned away by police. Now the best doctors in Timisoara were at her service. The mayor kept asking Laszlo to disperse the crowd.

By Saturday noon the almost carnival atmosphere had changed. Securitate agents moved through the crowd. They tried to provoke trouble. Mayor Mots now whistled a different tune. He turned on Laszlo, making all kinds of accusations against him. It was impossible to continue discussions with him, the mayor said. Laszlo's supporters jumped to his defense. They tried to make Mots promise to declare in writing that the pastor would not be evicted. But the mayor refused. The authorities stepped up the pressure. The fire brigade was called and lined up their hoses, poised to drench the crowd. The mayor phoned with an ultimatum: the demonstration must come to an end, or else.

By evening, the narrow street outside the church, as well as the roads all around, were thronged with thousands of people. Some just watched. Many others were horrified at the signs of the impending attack on Laszlo. "We love you! We love you!" they cried. "We will not leave! We will remain!" The people demanded that Laszlo conduct a service. They kept calling on him to come to the window and address them.

As darkness fell, the crowd sang a traditional Romanian folk song, the Dance of Unity. The first few bars took Laszlo by surprise. The song was sometimes sung by Romanian nationalists to express anti-Hungarian sentiments. At first it was not good music to his ears. But then pride swelled inside him, for he knew that the spirit of the crowd was not anti-Hungarian. As he listened, Laszlo felt this song was now a part of his own heritage. It had become to Laszlo a dance of Hungarian-Romanian solidarity. He listened with his hand on his heart.

Suddenly pandemonium broke out. Laszlo heard people shouting for the overthrow of the regime. "Down with the dictator! We want freedom!" Were these provocateurs? Would this be the excuse to bring in the troops? "Down with Ceausescu! We want free elections!" people shouted in unison. In tightly policed Romania, no one shouted such sentiments for long.

The animated crowd began to move off, much to Laszlo's relief. He feared that the growing anger could turn to violence. As revolutionary fervor spread, people began heading for the main square. They chanted and sang. More than 10,000 people packed the street leading to the town center. The whole town seemed to have sprung into action.

Between nine and ten in the evening, the army and the dreaded secret police, the Securitate, moved in to the town center with tanks and armored cars. The streets were full of officers with batons and helmets. The whole repressive apparatus was being drawn up for the attack. Shots rang out. Provocateurs began smashing shop windows, so the authorities could accuse the crowd of vandalism. Back at the church, the temperature was rising. Below Laszlo's window one man was shot. Laszlo and his wife saw the secret police repeatedly kick a young man as he lay on the ground, in case he was still alive. Laszlo wanted to rush down to help, but he was powerless.

Gunfire echoed all over the city. There was no way Laszlo and his wife could escape. The demonstration that had begun outside his window had left him behind. Police and demonstrators were battling it out elsewhere. It was a night of hell. Laszlo knew he could do nothing but wait for the final act. The authorities had their hands full for the moment. But they would return.

Six brave friends comforted Laszlo and Edith. They waited. They sat in the cold, miserable apartment. They had some supper. This was how the Last Supper must have felt, Laszlo thought. He thought of their three-year-old son, Mate, safe—he hoped—with Edith's parents in Dej. It was tranquil and silent in the flat. At three o'clock on Sunday morning, the peace was shattered as the front gate was brought down by a crash.

"Down With Ceausescu!"

The anger of the crowd shifted from the persecution of Tokes to all the crimes of the Ceausescu regime. The demonstration had worked up a momentum of its own. Years of suppressed hatred, anger and bitterness overcame the deeply entrenched fear of the repressive apparatus of a police state. Portraits of the hated dictator were ripped down. Bookshops with copies of his many books on display were wrecked. Demonstrators chanted, "Freedom!" "Down with Ceausescu!" and "We want bread!" The riot continued through the night. Troops attacked with tanks, fixed bayonets and water cannons. By 4:00 A.M. the crowds had been dispersed.

On Sunday morning, members of Laszlo's congregation arrived at the church. Debris from Saturday night's riot littered the pavement. A bus blocked the end of the street. Policemen let through only those who lived there. Members of the congregation met just around the corner. They gathered underneath a statue fifty yards away. Securitate officers in plainclothes came up to them in a group. There were about six of them, aged between thirty-five and forty. They moved through the crowd, taken aback by the strength and quiet determination. They looked uneasy, not knowing what might suddenly happen.

"We want to go to church," members of the crowd told them.

"There's no service," the Securitate replied.

"Our pastor should at least come to the window to tell us there is no service," the people insisted.

"He can't come to the window."

"Why not?"

"He's asleep."

"You expect us to believe that he's still asleep at nine thirty when the service is at ten o'clock?"

"He can't come, that's all."

By that time the people knew he was no longer there. Otherwise they would have brought Laszlo to the window.

An officer told one of the crowd Laszlo had gone.

"Where's he gone?"

"I don't know."

"But you must know!"

The officer got angry, increasingly eager to get rid of the troublesome crowd.

"Don't you understand you are playing with your freedom? You are good people. Go home, otherwise troublemakers will come and start breaking things."

The Securitate kept trying to move this crowd of about eighty away from the church. The whole time, people from the congregation were coming and going. They were tense and a bit frightened. They didn't know what would happen. The trolley car was ordered not to stop that day at the stop by the church.

A crowd of several thousand again took to the streets on Sunday afternoon, December 17. The weather was surprisingly warm. The people gathered outside the opera house on the main square. A few courageous ones climbed onto the balcony. This was to begin their week-long vigil there—they were afraid that if they came down they would be arrested.

Demonstrators converged on Timisoara's lightly guarded municipal buildings. They ransacked them in fury. Troops arrived and tried to disperse them. At about

2:00 P.M., five tanks and a helicopter appeared but did not at first open fire. The troops were attacked with stones and chairs by the unarmed crowd. The demonstrators refused to disperse and, about 4:00 P.M., more tanks and troops arrived, opening fire with machine guns.

The authorities were getting panicky. There was still one more week of university classes before the holidays, but the students were sent home early. An order went out that all student halls were to be cleared by noon on Tuesday. All students had to leave Timisoara by then.

No one in Timisoara, apart from the secret police, knew the whereabouts of Laszlo and his wife. People had seen them being bundled into cars and driven away in the darkness and confusion of the demonstrations. They knew the Tokeses would be shown no mercy. Local people, used to the barbaric ways of the Ceausescu regime, presumed that the two had been murdered. Protests poured in from around the world. The Prime Minister of Hungary expressed his concern. Laszlo's case was raised in many international organizations.

As the international protests mounted, Romania sealed itself off from the outside world. The borders with Hungary and Yugoslavia were virtually closed and only diplomats and businessmen were allowed into the country. The few foreign tourists who were allowed out had only confused stories of the dramatic events. A party of British schoolchildren on their way to a skiing trip in Romania was turned back.

The tightly controlled Romanian media made no mention of the uprising in Timisoara. But the Communist Party paper *Scinteia* cryptically warned that "all laws and regulations must be observed." And it threatened:

"Anyone who resists or refuses to obey the law must bear the consequences." The outside world could only piece together the picture of continuing protests from the few eyewitness reports that filtered out of the country. Romania's few international telephone lines were constantly jammed.

Hard, confirmed facts were hard to come by. But the unrest was spreading. The Timisoara demonstrations were followed by demonstrations in the nearby city of Arad and then in Brasov, the scene of the brutally repressed food riots in 1987. The uprising spread from west to east like a bushfire. The army was sent into town after town with tanks. Troops patrolled the main streets in Bucharest. Helicopters buzzed overhead. In Timisoara, demonstrators continued to pour out onto the streets. People ignored the 7:00 P.M.-to-8:00 A.M. curfew. Doctors worked around the clock in local hospitals to treat the wounded.

Vanished

The musician Ladislaus Csizmarik had spent Saturday evening practicing resistance songs with his choir: music in the service of the revolution. On Sunday he was shot, one of the first of the many victims in Timisoara. An unknown doctor came to Ladislaus's wife with the news. He had found the body in the morgue. He brought her his wedding ring and personal papers.

First thing next morning, the widow went to the hospital. Running battles were still raging in the streets. When she was let in, she learned the body of her husband had "vanished." All the other corpses, too, were gone.

"Where have they taken them? Where is he?" she cried.

On Sunday afternoon Zoltan Balaton discovered his daughter was among those with Laszlo and Edith on Saturday night. There was no trace of her or the others. What happened to her after the Securitate broke into Laszlo's church on Sunday morning? Had she been shot? Zoltan desperately wanted to learn the fate of his daughter.

Unbeknown to Zoltan, as Laszlo and Edith were dragged away in the darkness and bundled into cars, the six others were arrested as well. They were driven off at top speed to the Securitate headquarters in Timisoara. There they were taken down to the cellar and beaten. Lying on their stomachs, they were not allowed to look up. They never saw the faces of their savage attackers. The officers left the cellar. Someone then came in and kicked them. They lay there for about ten or fifteen hours—none of them knew how long.

They were then taken to the jail, where Zoltan's daughter was separated from the five men. Senior Securitate officers were brought in to question them. Each day they all had to endure a three- or four-hour "history lesson."

"Transylvania was never part of Hungary," they were told. "Hungarians are bandits." They all had to write a statement about what they were doing at Laszlo's home. "Laszlo Tokes is a traitor, a bandit. He is a dangerous madman." This was drummed into them.

At nine o'clock Wednesday morning, December 20, Zoltan got a phone call from a female colleague whose husband worked for the Securitate. She told Zoltan that his daughter was being held by the secret police. Zoltan breathed a deep sigh of relief. His daughter was alive but not out of danger. She must be saved, he thought.

Zoltan acted quickly. By lunchtime he had gathered a crowd of several hundred of his students and led them to the party headquarters. A big crowd was already there. Zoltan addressed them, calling on them to demand his daughter's freedom and freedom for Laszlo's other brave friends. The army stood on the sidelines, unwilling to intervene. The crowd prevented the local party leaders from leaving until the six were freed. Now the party leaders were themselves hostages. They yielded and released the six captives that evening.

Country Captivity

Sunday morning, December 17. Laszlo woke from his fitful sleep. His fear subsided somewhat as he could see that the cars were sticking together. At dawn, he could sense they were heading northeast. A familiar landmark here and there revealed the direction. They were driving through the gently rolling hills of the Salaj district. The convoy passed wretched villages and shabbily dressed peasants toiling away at their medieval agriculture. The country looked beautiful in the cold early morning sunshine.

The cars veered off the main road onto a bumpy farm track. Laszlo realized his destination was the village of Mineu, the place of banishment chosen months before by his bishop, in collusion with the government.

Finally they arrived in the remote village. A small crowd was waiting by the church. The police came toward the car without saying a word. Laszlo and his wife were hustled into the derelict parsonage. No pastor had lived

31

in Mineu for years. The primitive house was cold and had no running water.

The regional dean of the Reformed Church was on hand to meet them. The police had roused him from his slumber at 4:00 A.M. with instructions to welcome the new pastor to his post. A guard ordered Laszlo to wash his face. It would not do for a congregation to receive a blood-stained pastor. Laszlo obeyed.

By dawn the police had raised a wire fence around the dwelling. The country cottage was now a prison camp. The police brought in dogs. Police, Securitate agents and members of the Romanian national guard all took turns watching the Tokeses. They installed bright lights that shone into the house night and day. They secretly planted a listening device to catch their every word.

Laszlo and Edith were completely cut off from the outside world. Had the demonstrations already been crushed? How many people had been killed?

A truck arrived with some of the family's few possessions. There were some hastily gathered clothes. Bits of broken furniture. Even some food. Everything was all mixed up. But Laszlo found three radios. He seized them with joy and smuggled them into the house wrapped up in old clothes. Now they could listen to them secretly to find out what had happened in Timisoara. He immediately hid two, in case they were confiscated, and stuffed the third into an old pillow. With one ear to the speaker, he switched it on. It worked!

The news from the outside world was overwhelming. On Saturday evening the first news of the uprising in Timisoara had leaked out of the country. Even in tightly controlled Romania, the government could not stop the spread of news about such a momentous event—thanks to foreign broadcasts. As they sat hunched over the radio, listening to Hungarian radio, Radio Free Europe from Munich and the BBC, the couple rejoiced that the demonstrations were continuing. Laszlo was especially heartened to hear of worldwide support for them. Laszlo and Edith now had hope.

Laszlo supported Edith, who had lurched from what he feared was the verge of a breakdown to exhilaration at the sheer joy of being alive. Over the radio they heard reports that they had been killed. Then other stations said they were in Mineu, while others claimed they had been taken to the far side of the country. Laszlo feared the strain on his delicate wife would bring about a miscarriage.

Timisoara, Monday, December 18. Demonstrations continued. No one knew who was on which side. Shots were fired in all directions. Some streets were quiet and deserted. Others were thronged with confused and excited people. Security forces on the main square started shooting at demonstrators. People fled in all directions in panic. The Orthodox Metropolitan Nicolae ordered the doors of his cathedral closed to prevent people from taking refuge. He would have no part in this uprising.

On Tuesday there was shooting at Timisoara's Elektro-Banat factory. In every Romanian factory the Communist workers organization had a well-stocked armory. The army went in to try to take away these weapons, to keep them from falling into the hands of the demonstrators. But the workers refused to allow the soldiers into the factories. They stood guarding the gates; the soldiers on the other side drew up with tanks. As the army shot at a woman and her child, the Elektro-Banat factory went on strike. The army sealed off the plant, posting sentries all around.

As the two sides watched each other tensely, other factories joined the strike. One chemical factory threatened that, if the soldiers moved into the Elektro-Banat works, they would blow up the plant. That would be enough to destroy the whole city.

Workers came streaming from their factories to join those already on the main square. As evening fell, people brought tea and food for the crowds, especially the defiant leaders on the balcony of the opera house.

Wednesday, December 20. The crowds on the streets of Timisoara reached 50,000. The demonstrators demanded the return of the bodies of those shot by the security forces. No one knew how many had died. Early reports spoke of thousands. (Later it emerged that the true figure was nearly 200.) Rumors ran wild. Everyone believed that the Securitate had hastily buried bodies in unmarked mass graves. Workers at the Autoturism car factory tore down a huge portrait of Ceausescu adorning the factory gates and put up black ribbons as a sign of mourning for those who had died. Workers from here and from other factories dropped their tools and joined the mass demonstrations.

In the face of the crowd's fury, the army ceased fire. Soldiers who only a few days before had been shooting at demonstrators looked on passively. In other cities, too, soldiers refused orders to open fire. Open conflict appeared between different units of the government forces.

This was the turning point for the Timisoara uprising.

Virtually everyone overcame their fear. Now the army, made up mostly of drafted men, refused further orders to crack down. The determination to oust the hated Communist regime could not be stopped. The people saw they could win. They knew their goal would be achieved only through sacrifice. An end was in sight to the years of silent suffering.

In Timisoara, the "cradle of the revolution," the protesters gradually formed themselves into an organization. In the chaos of revolution, a Committee of the Democratic Front was born. The Romanian government had cracked down so harshly on all forms of dissent that no organized opposition group had been able to operate underground for long. Dissidents were arrested and isolated before they could organize themselves. No Romanian equivalent of Czechoslovakia's Civic Forum or East Germany's New Forum existed, both of which had channeled feelings of hatred against dictatorship into organized action.

The leaders of the chaotic protest movement in Timisoara consisted of clergymen and spontaneously chosen representatives. Paul Negrut, a visiting Baptist pastor from Oradea, addressed the huge crowds in the main square. Standing on the balcony of the former party offices, he urged the people to work for peaceful change in society.

Wednesday evening, December 20. Timisoara had declared itself a free city. The demonstrators waited for news of uprisings elsewhere. Candles burned outside the cathedral and in other places where protesters had been shot. A bus still blocked off the street leading to Laszlo Tokes's house and church. Tanks and soldiers prevented anyone from approaching. No one knew where the Tokeses were.

Interrogation

Laszlo and Edith had spent two days in relative peace. But on Tuesday the 19th, interrogations had begun. Special Securitate members were brought in. The leader of the group came from distant Bucharest. The two were carted off to the local council offices of the militia headquarters in the nearby town of Zalau for interrogation. Husband and wife were always interrogated separately. They had to endure long hours of hostile questioning.

The leader of the interrogation crew was beastly. While Laszlo wrote his statements, the Securitate chief lounged with his feet on the table reading cheap bestsellers. He occasionally interrupted his reading to shout crude abuse. Laszlo wrote forty or fifty pages during the three days of interrogation. The Securitate official from time to time tried to give the image of a cultured man, but Laszlo had no doubt that he could suddenly turn and break his neck.

The interrogators tried to extract confessions. They were gathering evidence for a show trial. They wanted to portray Laszlo before the country and the world as the instigator of a plan to overthrow the whole system in Romania. He was accused of being in the pay of reactionary western countries—especially Hungary. They said he was a Judas who had accepted dollars, cocoa, cigarettes and other scarce goods to betray his country. They alternated harsh threats with moments of softness. But they did not beat either Laszlo or Edith. She became bolder and recovered the power to resist.

Day after day, the pressure was stepped up. The interrogators said confession was the only way Laszlo and

Edith could save their lives. Laszlo refused point-blank. The intensified pressure weighed heavily on his spirits. On Thursday, as the interrogation seemed to be reaching its climax, Laszlo begged for one more day to think over his decision—he had to play for time. His persecutors agreed.

On Friday morning, while waiting for the Securitate convoy that turned up each morning to take him to Zalau, Laszlo heard that Ceausescu had declared a state of emergency. This could mean anything. Perhaps the Ceausescus' days were numbered, or perhaps they were on the verge of mounting a decisive counteroffensive. Whatever the case, Laszlo felt helpless. He and Edith were completely in their clutches. What might the desperate regime do now?

TWO

The Land, the People, the Church

Laszlo Tokes was born on April 1, 1952, in the historic city of Cluj. Occupying a strategic position on the sloping banks of the Somersul Mic (Kis Szamos) River, Cluj was the site of a thriving metropolis in Roman times. The Roman conquerors called it Napoca. (Cluj was renamed Cluj-Napoca in 1974 to revive the memory of the town's ancient past.) After the withdrawal of the Romans in 271 A.D., barbarians from the East razed the town. The place remained desolate long afterward. The origins of the present city go back to the twelfth century, when King Bela III built a fortress on the ruins of old Napoca. Over the years Cluj prospered and expanded. By the fifteenth century, it had become the dynamic cultural and economic capital of Transylvania.

To understand Laszlo Tokes, you have to understand Transylvania. The issues that brought Laszlo to fame have to do with the deep and fascinating history of his homeland. "A strange little country is this Transylvania! Very likely the reader never heard its name before." So observed the eccentric English writer and scholar John Paget after completing an exhaustive tour of the remote country in 1839. One hundred and fifty years later Transylvania remains a strange land of striking contrasts and contradictions. On this small patch of Eastern Europe, no greater in size than Virginia, Asiatic and Western ways coexist side by side. Breathtaking natural beauty and irreversible despoliation of the environment make up the landscape. An uplifting Christian spirituality and a barbaric paganism compete for the hearts and minds of the people. Ramshackle hovels and decaying concrete-and-steel apartment blocks stand in the shadow of majestic cathedrals and romantic castles. The traveler encounters both unrivaled hospitality and unwelcoming suspicion.

Undoubtedly, more people in the late twentieth century have heard of Transylvania than in John Paget's day. After all, Paget wrote well before Hollywood made Transylvania a household name as the setting of Count Dracula films. But, apart from legends of vampires and werewolves, few English speakers know much more about faraway Transylvania than in the mid-nineteenth century.

Together with the former principalities of Moldavia and Wallachia to the east, Transylvania forms present-day Romania. Transylvania is separated from the two ex-principalities by the craggy heights of the Carpathian mountains, which form a semicircle around her eastern flank. The deep snows of the Carpathians feed the many rivers and streams that traverse the arable fields, meadows, orchards and forests as they flow westward toward the arid Hungarian plain.

The aura of a bygone age envelops most of the countryside. The pace of life is slow. The workhorse still competes with the tractor and the scythe with the harvester. Chickens, dogs and goats leisurely roam the mud streets of Transylvania's dilapidated villages. But here and there the rustic charm gives way to the environmental monstrosities of Ceausescu's brave new world—the notoriously soul-destroying agro-industrial complexes. Transylvania's large towns—Cluj, Brasov, Timisoara and Oradea—all boast medieval churches, baroque palaces and art deco public buildings. But these relics of a more prosperous past are ringed by drab and decaying apartment blocks, inspired by the uninspiring "socialist realist" school of architecture imported from the Soviet Union.

Transylvania has been a part of Romania for less than seventy-five years. At the end of World War I, the Romanian army occupied Transylvania. Its incorporation into the Romanian state was sanctioned two years later by the Treaty of Trianon. For over 900 years beforehand, Transylvania was a land of the Hungarian crown. Hungary's first king, St. Stephen, conquered the territory in 1003 A.D., firmly bringing it into the Hungarian political orbit. But its remoteness from the center of Hungarian government on the Danube meant Transylvania enjoyed local self-government and its own administration for much of its history. For nearly 200 years following the decisive Turkish defeat of the Hungarian army in the swamps of Mohacs in 1526, Transylvania was virtually an independent country and played an important role in European affairs.

When the Habsburgs drove the Islamic Turks out of Hungary at the end of the seventeenth century, Transylvania and all the other Hungarian crown lands were reunited under one Habsburg monarch. Transylvania continued to be governed differently from the other Hungarian crown lands till the age of nationalism. In the nineteenth century, the Hungarian ruling class wished to create a centralized state out of Hungary and Transylvania. The union of Transylvania and Hungary was one of their demands in Hungary's revolution of 1848. The dream of the Hungarian elite was fulfilled in 1868. Transylvania lost its constitutional distinctiveness and local self-government as it was united with Hungary.

Hungary, as an ally of imperial Germany, found herself on the losing side of the First World War. Part of the heavy price was the loss of historic Transylvania and a broad strip of eastern Hungary to Romania. Transylvania never regained self-government. Under Romanian rule, she was merged into a centralized state that failed to respect her ancient history and traditions, especially those of the Hungarian minority.

Transylvania is both blessed and bedeviled by a host of nationalities. The overwhelming majority—roughly 65 percent—speak Romanian as their mother tongue. About one-quarter of the people identify themselves as Hungarians. Germans and Jews once had a strong and visible presence in the land. Both groups left a big mark on the country's cultural and economic development. But the Holocaust virtually wiped out the Jews. Most of the wretched survivors emigrated to Israel or the United

States. Their synagogues now stand empty and decaying, their cemeteries buried beneath weeds and brambles.

The West German government struck a deal with the Ceausescu regime whereby ransom money—reputed to be 10,000 marks per person (more than $6000)—would be paid to secure the right of tens of thousands of German-descended Romanians to emigrate to Germany. Thus the young, healthy and fit Germans and Jews have tended to take the opportunity to leave Transylvania. So depleted are these two communities that their future existence is now in doubt. Small numbers of Slovaks, Ukrainians and Serbs have also managed to preserve their national identities. Transylvania is also the home of hundreds of thousands of Gypsies. As in other East European nations, the Gypsies are openly mistrusted and hated.

Oil and Water

The nationalities of Transylvania mix like oil and water. Though close neighbors, they have been separated for centuries by language, culture, religion and law. The attitude of the nationalities toward each other ranges from indifference and patronizing contempt to open hatred. One hundred and fifty years ago, John Paget noted with surprise that intermarriage between the Hungarians and Romanians of the same village was virtually unknown. Instances of personal friendship, understanding and even marriage between people of different nationalities do occur. But heartfelt love and cooperation is rarely found at the community level.

Relations between the nationalities tend to be best in cosmopolitan towns where more than two nationalities coexist. The town of Timisoara in the southeast corner of the country is a case in point. There four major nationalities—Romanians, Germans, Hungarians and Serbs—have lived together in relative peace, each unable to entertain hopes of entirely dominating the others. The prevailing harmony of the nationalities was an important factor in the town's united support for Laszlo Tokes. But towns like Timisoara are exceptions rather than the rule.

From time to time the nationalities have collectively joined forces, usually in a wild and spontaneous explosion against a common enemy. This happened on the night of December 15 in Timisoara when Romanians, Hungarians and Germans took to the streets to bring down the hated Ceausescu regime. But in most cases the old alienating instincts quickly resurface once the bolt of cooperation has been shot. As in Lebanon and Northern Ireland, national reconciliation remains an unfulfilled dream in Transylvania.

Relations between Hungarians and Romanians began a sharp downward slide at the end of the nineteenth century. The Hungarian government initiated a chauvinistic policy of Hungarianization. This extended the use of Hungarian in schools, the courts and administration. It was accompanied by shrill crowing about the glories of Hungarian civilization. Notwithstanding the fanfare, Hungarianization failed miserably. But it did succeed in raising the hackles of the Romanian people. After World War I, the tables were turned. The Romanian government paid the Hungarians back in kind. Romanian chauvinism was a bitter pill for the Hungarians to swallow.

Relations turned violently ugly during World War II, when Hitler divided Transylvania between Hungary and Romania, then both fascist allies of the Third Reich. Inhuman atrocities were committed by Hungarians against Romanians in the north of the country under Hungarian rule. Hungarians experienced the same at the hands of Romanians in the south. Villages were razed by both sides. A large number of Hungarian-speaking Szeklers were summarily executed by the Romanians, and Hungarians in return instituted pogroms against Romanians.

Three Privileged Nations

Theories abound, but the origins of the Romanian people are shrouded in mystery. However, no doubt exists about the roots of their language. Romanian is a Romance language, closely related to Latin, French and Italian—a fact of which Romanians are enormously proud. Latin was brought to Transylvania by the Romans in the second century A.D. when they conquered the territory then know as Dacia. The small Roman settlements there existed for less than two centuries before the Romans withdrew, leaving Dacia open to wave after wave of barbarian invasions. In the ensuing chaos, virtually every remnant of Roman civilization was obliterated from the area. But in some mysterious way that archeologists, linguists and historians have never been able to explain satisfactorily, the basic patterns of the Latin language survived and evolved into modern Romanian. Moreover, the language spread across the Carpathians to Moldavia and Wallachia, where the Romans never had a permanent presence, to become the mother tongue of 20 million Romanian people.

The Hungarians are relative newcomers to Europe. Nomadic Hungarian tribesmen penetrated the Carpathians at the end of the ninth century. Their ancestral homeland was east of the Ural Mountains in western Siberia. The language, customs and appearance of the Hungarian invaders were Asiatic rather than European. Their linguistic relatives, the Vogul and the Ostyak tribes, still live as nomads in northern Russia. Not only were the native people of the Carpathian basin terrorized by the Hungarian hordes, ancient chronicles also tell of murderous Hungarian horsemen plundering towns and villages across all of Europe. The Hungarians quickly occupied the Danubian plain in what is present-day Hungary. But, protected by the rough terrain, the rulers of Transylvania were able to resist Hungarian rule for over a century till the reign of St. Stephen. The hold of St. Stephen's successors on Transylvania was slippery. The Hungarian invaders were not numerous enough to populate and defend their easternmost possession against the fierce Tartars and Cumans beyond the Carpathians.

In the twelfth century, Hungarian kings invited foreign colonists to Transylvania. The Szekely tribe was the first to come. They were granted lands in the eastern bend of the Carpathians and special noble status. In return they were obliged to defend the frontier from invaders. The medieval town of Tirgu Mures (Marosvasarhely) is the historic capital of the Szekely territory. No one knows the ethnic background of this tribe. Some scholars believe they were close relatives of the Hungarians. Whatever the case, they were speaking Hungarian as their mother tongue from an early date. Today the Szekely people are often thought of as more Hungarian than the Hungarians. They have kept alive ancient customs and speech patterns that have long since disappeared from the everyday life of modern Hungarians.

Germans were also enticed to settle in Transylvania shortly after the Szekelys. These Germans, who later became known as the Saxons, received self-government and tax-exempt status. The kings of Hungary were not only interested in the Saxons' military service. They were also eager for the Germans' highly developed technical skills and business acumen to be transplanted to Transylvania. Even today, visitors to Brasov are instantly struck by the Germanic look of the town center.

Transylvania was politically dominated by the so-called "three privileged nations" for most of its history. These "nations" were the Hungarian nobility, the Szekelys and the Saxons. When the kings of Hungary called together the Transylvanian assembly, these three groups were represented. The rest of the population—the Hungarian and Romanian peasantry—were excluded. They had no political rights and had to pay all the taxes. Most subsisted as serfs, bound to the land and obliged to perform backbreaking labor for ungrateful lords. In the middle ages, the nobles of Transylvania were tyrannical by European standards. While feudalism in England, France and Germany was gradually breaking down, it was intensifying in Transylvania. The lot of the common peasant was deteriorating.

In 1514, the peasants of Hungary and Transylvania rose in revolt against the excesses of their masters. The peasants' leader was a brave but unsophisticated Szekely army officer named Gyorgy Dozsa. Dozsa was captured following a bloody battle on the outskirts of Timisoara. His captors wished to teach the ungrateful peasants a lesson that would never be forgotten. Dozsa was taken in chains to Timisoara's town square, where he was barbarically executed. He was thrust upon a red-hot throne. A red-hot crown was mockingly forced upon his head while molten lead was poured into his eye sockets. Dozsa's followers were forced to eat scorched flesh torn from his writhing body as a prelude to their own gruesome demise. Afterward, the enslavement of the peasantry became more severe than ever. As late as the middle of the last century, Transylvanian serfs had to serve their lords two to three days a week without pay. Twenty-five lashes could be administered on the spot to any serf who incurred the displeasure of his master. John Paget tells of meeting a Hungarian countess who customarily expected her serfs to prostrate themselves in the mud to save her shoes from being soiled.

Serfdom was abolished in 1848—seventeen years before the Emancipation Proclamation in the United States. But, as in the American South, freedom from servitude did not necessarily bring dramatic improvements in living conditions. Economic and political power remained in the hands of the "three privileged nations." Illiteracy and grinding poverty remained the order of the day for many Transylvanian peasants.

The Romanian peasants had a double disadvantage. Not only were they subjected along with the Hungarian plebs to the evils of serfdom but the "three privileged nations" also conspired to suppress their national aspirations. The ruling classes feared the numerous Romanians, seeing them as a potential fifth column inside the country. It was suspected that the real political and religious loyalty of the Romanian people was commanded by Romanian princes and Orthodox prelates beyond the Carpathians, who would use these peasants to overturn the political and religious order of the country.

The Romanians on both sides of the Carpathians were almost exclusively Eastern Orthodox, whereas the Hungarians, Germans and Szekelys were mainly Catholics and Protestants. The spiritual allegiance of the Romanian people historically lay not with the Pope or bishops approved by the Transylvanian ruling classes but with hierarchs of the Greek and Bulgarian Churches. Thus, for centuries, the Romanians were barred from having any political institutions that might promote their national aspirations, and the Orthodox Church, while not banned, endured disadvantages.

Good News for Transylvania

The Gospel was first proclaimed in Transylvania by Roman colonists. What happened to Christianity after the end of the Roman occupation of Dacia is obscure. By the ninth century, missionaries from Constantinople and the Bulgarian Empire were making inroads into Transylvania. They brought with them the Cyrillic alphabet and, above all, the Eastern liturgy still used today in the Orthodox Church. Before long, Western religious influences had also reached Transylvania via Hungary. In the year 1000 A.D., the politically astute St. Stephen of Hungary accepted the Holy Crown from Pope Sylvester II and immediately began establishing Roman Catholic dioceses throughout his realm. He established two in present-day Transylvania: one in Oradea (Nagyvarad), the other in Alba Iulia (Gyulafehervar).

Thereafter the Church of Rome and its Latin liturgy enjoyed a strong advantage in Transylvania, gradually becoming the ascendant tradition. Roman Catholicism became the religion of the Hungarians and the Szekelys. The Germans brought their Catholic faith with them to Transylvania. But the Romanians resisted the Western variety of Christianity. They remained loyal to the Eastern liturgy and the Orthodox Church. Ironically, while the Asiatic Hungarians were now adopting Western ways, the Latin-tongued Romanians clung to the spiritual traditions of the East.

Catholicism and Orthodoxy remained unchallenged in Transylvania until the Reformation. The sound of Luther's hammer on the door of the Wittenberg Castle Chapel in 1517 soon reverberated throughout Transylvania. After much religious and political strife, Protestantism prevailed among the Hungarians, Szekelys and Germans. Less than a century after the beginning of the Reformation, only a handful of Catholic priests remained in the land. The two bishoprics were vacant. The Lutheran creeds found fertile ground among the Saxon townsmen. The Reformed and Unitarian Churches won the hearts and minds of the Hungarians and Szekelys. The Reformed Church in particular was so closely identified with the Hungarian community that it became known simply as "the Hungarian faith."

The Protestants organized missions to convert the Orthodox Romanians. Bibles and Protestant tracts were published in Romanian. An ethnic Romanian synod of the Reformed Church was established and a former Orthodox priest elected the country's first Romanian Reformed Bishop. But all this missionary zeal made little impact on the mass of the Romanian people, who remained true to their familiar Orthodox liturgy.

Transylvania was fortunate to escape some of the worst excesses of the Reformation. The religiously divided "three privileged nations" saw their self-interests served by tolerance for the Catholic, Reformed, Lutheran and Unitarian Churches. In 1571 the Transylvanian assembly declared these churches "received" denominations. This meant that their freedom to function was guaranteed by law. But the Orthodox Church and other groups deemed potentially subversive, such as the Anabaptists, remained outside this arrangement. The Orthodox Church had a second-class status as a mere "tolerated" church. Its freedom to operate depended on the whim of the authorities.

Roman Catholicism made a remarkable comeback at the end of the seventeenth century, during the Counter-Reformation. The Catholic renewal was inextricably bound up with the rise of Habsburg power in Transylvania, following the ouster of the Turks from Hungary. The Habsburg dynasty was stridently Catholic. It aimed to forge together a vast empire in Central Europe made up of many lands and peoples. The Catholic Church, according to the Habsburg vision, would bind the motley empire together spiritually and culturally around the Habsburg throne. Zealous missionary efforts and anti-Protestant policies enabled the Catholic Church to again rival the Protestant Churches among the Hungarians, Szekelys and Germans. Like the Protestant churches during the Reformation, the Catholic Church tried to make inroads among the Orthodox Romanians, only with much more success.

Scarcely had the Habsburgs stamped their royal authority on Transylvania when they sent Jesuit missionaries there to lure the Orthodox to unite with the Roman Catholic Church. The Habsburgs were prepared to make a deal with the Orthodox. In return for transferring their allegiance away from the Patriarch in Constantinople to the Pope in Rome, the Orthodox would be allowed to retain their Eastern liturgy and married priests. Moreover, they would receive equal legal status with the "received" denominations. Thus, for the first time in the history of Transylvania, a Romanian national institution enjoyed freedoms guaranteed by law. The Orthodox hierarchy accepted this offer, and most of the priests and the faithful followed suit. This peculiar branch of the Catholic Church became known as the Eastern-rite or the Uniate Church. The Eastern-rite Catholic Church thereafter became instrumental in the development of Romanian national consciousness in Transylvania.

The smaller evangelical churches, such as the Baptists, Adventists, Brethren and Pentecostals, took root in Transylvania within the last 100 years. The largest of these churches—the Baptist Church—was founded as a result of Hungarian and German missionary activity. The "peasant prophet" Mihaly Kornya won thousands of converts as he traveled by bicycle from village to village preaching the need for personal conversion and commitment. The Baptist faith quickly spread from the Hungarian and German communities to the Romanian people.

Though relatively small in number, the evangelical

churches have become a dynamic and influential spiritual force in the country. Their success encouraged evangelical renewal movements in the old established churches, such as the Orthodox Lord's Army and the Protestant interdenominational Bethany Movement. The activists of the small evangelical churches often faced harassment by the authorities, who were sometimes encouraged to act by jealous leaders of the privileged churches. Preachers could not preach legally without a license issued by the state. Public revival meetings were frequently broken up by the police.

THREE

Formative Years

A hard winter was giving way to spring as young Laszlo took his first breath and notified the world of his arrival with a loud cry. A large, loving family was on hand to welcome the newest member of the expanding Tokes clan. Laszlo's parents, Istvan and Erzsebet, had already been married for eleven years. Laszlo was their seventh child, the fourth boy.

Istvan and Erzsebet met one summer at a Reformed Church youth conference on the outskirts of Cluj. It was love at first sight. Erzsebet was struck by the confidence and dignity of Istvan as the up-and-coming seminary student expounded upon the Scriptures. The lively eyes and quick smile of the petite Erzsebet left a deep impression on the heart of Istvan.

But marriage had to wait. Istvan was committed to begin postgraduate theology studies at Tubingen in Germany in the fall of 1939, the year of the outbreak of World War II. The young Hungarian scholar did not find the totalitarian atmosphere of Nazi Germany congenial. After a term at Tubingen, Istvan went to Switzerland. He spent a semester in Basel, where he studied under renowned Reformed theologian Karl Barth. Barth's teaching had a powerful effect on Istvan. Barth had gained fame for shifting the theological direction of his Church away from liberalism and toward a more biblically based, orthodox outlook. He sympathized with evangelical renewal movements. But for the German theologian, conversion did not end with a simple personal decision for Christ. Conversion, he believed, marked the beginning of the Christian's pilgrimage through life—a pilgrimage that brought the believer face-to-face with tough personal, social, ecclesiastical and political questions. For Barth, the Christian life meant involvement in, rather than retreat from, the world.

At first Barth was not inclined to confront the Nazis directly. But eventually he became so convinced of the demonic nature of Hitler and the Nazi creed that political neutrality was out of the question. Barth became a bold opponent of Nazism and its sinister influence on the German Protestant Churches. He left Germany in 1935, after his refusal to take an oath of loyalty to the Nazi state brought him into conflict with the authorities.

Istvan returned to Cluj in 1940, taking back with him the Barthian tradition—a tradition that would provide a sound theological underpinning for the stormy days ahead.

Istvan and Erzsebet's romance was unbroken by Istvan's sojourn in Germany and Switzerland. Erzsebet, too, had traveled to Germany to work as an *au pair*. The couple did not meet abroad, but they continued a voluminous correspondence. They were married soon after their return to Cluj. Istvan took up work as the secretary to the Reformed Bishop of Cluj, Janos Vasarhelyi. Their first child, Erzsebet, was born in 1941. Seven more followed in quick succession.

These were lean years for Istvan and Erzsebet. Their world was cruelly topsy-turvy. Their hopes for a better future were raised in 1940 when the Vienna Award restored northern Transylvania, including Cluj, to Hungary. But these were soon dashed when Hungary was occupied by the German army and power was seized by Hungarian Nazis. Calamity after calamity seemed to befall Transylvania. The bloody Nazi rule was brought to an end by advancing Soviet troops in 1944. But the Red Army wreaked its own variety of havoc wherever it went. Erzsebet was forced to flee Cluj to give birth to her daughter Anna in the countryside, as the Soviets advanced on the city.

The Red Army brought with it a new political order. Hopes of real liberation were dashed as the Red Army imposed Communist domination. Society was in turmoil as the Soviet-backed Romanian government brutally embarked on madcap schemes: the collectivization of agriculture, the nationalization of industry and the elimination of political opposition. Social and economic life was in chaos. The Romanian Communist Party pursued a vigorous campaign against religion. Many restrictions were placed on the churches. Before long, legal church activity could take place only on church premises. The government went so far as to ban the 1.5-million-strong

Eastern-rite Catholic Church and evangelical renewal movements, such as the dynamic interdenominational Christian Endeavor (Bethany) and the Orthodox Lord's Army. Hundreds of priests and pastors disappeared. Some were found later, murdered. Others ended up in prisons or labor camps.

One day in 1950, Istvan was visited by an official of the government's Department of Religious Affairs, which controlled the churches. "You're a Hitlerite," the man accused him. Istvan was mystified. The official pointed to what he believed was a swastika in the Church yearbook he edited. Istvan explained that it was a reproduction of fifteenth-century traditional needlework and that the whole yearbook had been approved by the censor in Bucharest. His protestations were in vain. Istvan was arrested and spent two months in jail in Cluj. He was lucky to emerge with his life and health intact.

Lenin Boulevard

Istvan and Erzsebet established their home on Lenin Boulevard in 1945. Their high-ceilinged, nineteenth-century apartment with its traditional wood-burning ceramic stove had almost a stately aura about it. Upon the Tokeses' arrival, the three-room apartment seemed spacious and airy. But by the time Laszlo arrived seven years later, it had become crowded and cramped. Laszlo and his seven siblings slept, played and did their homework in one room. Bunk beds were a necessity, with one against each wall of the living room. Istvan's book-lined study was a no-go area for the children, but they had free rein in the kitchen and the other two rooms.

Physical survival might have been impossible for the young Tokes family were it not for Istvan's colleagues and friends, who gave of their own meager surplus to keep the family provisioned. Meals were simple. Breakfast usually consisted of bread and plum jam. The children had milk courtesy of a local farmer who delivered eight pints each day to the Tokes household. Erzsebet did all in her power to provide the family with one hot meal a day. Most of the time it amounted to no more than beans or potatoes. The children would become excited on those rare festive occasions when meat or eggs graced the kitchen table. Erzsebet recalls feeding an apple to the infant Laszlo with all the other children vying with each other to get the peeling, like a brood of baby sparrows competing for a worm. To make ends meet, Erzsebet took in home knitting on a piecework basis. Istvan became the family's shoemaker.

Despite the hard times, Istvan and Erzsebet chose to have many children. Having children was a conscious act of faith in a loving God. They believed that God had given them something precious—something they wanted to pass on to their own children—the love of Jesus Christ. Istvan and Erzsebet trusted that God would work through each of their offspring to make the world, in some small way, a better place. But they never imagined in their wildest dreams that God would choose young Laszlo to make such a dramatic and positive impact on the course of history.

Only a strong faith could have given the young couple this sense of optimism. Cold reason might have led them to a desperate attempt to flee the country or perhaps suicidal despair. But they were not the sort of Christians to pay mere lip service to the words of Jesus: "So do not worry, saying, 'What shall we eat?' or 'What shall we drink?' or 'What shall we wear?' For the pagans run after all these things, and your heavenly Father knows that you need them. But seek first his kingdom and his righteousness, and all these things will be given to you as well" (Matthew 6:31–33). Istvan and Erzsebet made this teaching a reality in their daily lives. When asked today if she regrets having had so many children, considering the difficulties they brought with them, Erzsebet's answer is an emphatic no. "There is nothing more beautiful," she testifies, "than to point to eight respectable children who love each other and who stick together through thick and thin."

Istvan and Erzsebet were materially poor, but they had intellectual and spiritual treasures to offer their young ones. Both parents had lively minds and fascinating personalities. In many ways Istvan and Erzsebet were opposites. But their different characters created a healthy harmony rather than destructive conflict. Istvan was a thoughtful, pensive scholar of Szekely stock. He descended from a long line of Reformed pastors. His children remember him for his levelheadedness, nerves of steel and puritan disposition. Istvan had a winning way of passing on profound spiritual truths to his offspring in a simple, intelligible way. The intellectual powers of Laszlo were largely forged by Istvan. So, too, were Laszlo's political instincts. Working at the headquarters of Transylvania's Reformed Church, Istvan was steeped in Church politics that were tightly intertwined with national politics. Young Laszlo often overheard fascinating conversations between Istvan and his most trusted colleagues about political affairs.

Erzsebet was more spirited, expressive and artistic than Istvan. She was born of peasant stock and was raised in the rural Mezoseg region between Cluj and the Szekely country. Her father was a first-generation Reformed pastor. He remained close to the soil during his ministry. His special mission was to provide basic education for the poor Hungarian and Romanian children of nearby villages. Having come from an area of mixed nationality, unlike Istvan, Erzsebet was more acutely aware than her husband of the wide gulf that separated Hungarians from Romanians. Her boundless enthusiasm for Hungarian customs and folklore was passed on to young Laszlo.

Erzsebet adored the verse of the young Hungarian poets of Transylvania, who after the separation from Hungary powerfully expressed the lamentation of the Hungarian spirit. In her favorite poem, "Psalmus Hungaricus," Jeno Dsida took as his inspiration Psalm 137. He compared the situation of the Hungarians in Romania to that of the captive Jews in Babylon.

By the waters of Babylon:
If I forget thee,
let my water turn to wormwood!
When my tongue speaks not of thee,
let an incandescent nail pierce it!
If I cease to gaze upon thee,
let the light of my eyes darken!
My people, you are holy, you are cursed, but precious!

Over and over again the words of this refrain filled the ears and touched the heart of Laszlo.

A Golden Age

Laszlo's education began quite literally at his mother's knee.

The family kitchen was Laszlo's first schoolroom. Erzsebet had a gift for doing two or more jobs at once. While she scrubbed the floor or peeled the potatoes, she sang songs, recited poetry and told tales to Laszlo. Most of all he loved to hear about the heroic acts and cunning diplomacy of Gabor Bethlen, the Reformed Prince of Transylvania, in the early seventeenth century. Prince Bethlen presided over what the Hungarians call the "golden age" of Transylvania. The Prince secured the independence of the country by defeating the German Habsburgs on the battlefield and by paying tribute to the Islamic Turks. His foreign policy created the conditions for domestic peace for the first time in many decades.

Prince Bethlen was renowned for governing according to the rule of law and practicing religious tolerance. But what made Laszlo particularly proud of this Hungarian prince was his devout Calvinism. Prince Bethlen was reputed to read his Bible daily and he vigorously defended and generously patronized Transylvanian Protestantism. Raised in what he calls the "Bethlen tradition," Laszlo still considers this Transylvanian prince an inspiration.

The horizons of the Tokes children were broadened by the Church. Each Sunday the family would stroll past the opera house and the former Eastern-rite Catholic Cathedral to the fifteenth-century Reformed Church in Farkas Street. The pastor, the Reverend Laszlo Dezso, was a good friend of Istvan and one of the most dynamic pastors of his generation. He had spent some hard years in a labor camp soon after the Soviet occupation of Romania. Pastor Dezso and his wife Eva ran the Sunday school. The pastor was a fantastic storyteller and Aunt Eva, as the children called her, an imaginative musician. They held the Tokes children spellbound. The Dezsos had to be gifted to succeed. The Communist state forbade the publication of Sunday school workbooks and teaching material. Whatever they used was from the pre-war period.

Poverty did not prevent Laszlo the city-boy from experiencing rural life. The family did not have the means for expensive vacations. But Istvan's colleagues often welcomed the company of the Tokes children when they were called to preach in the countryside. Laszlo often set off with Pastor Janos Herman, who, though physically frail, lived something of a nomadic life, wandering from village to village preaching the Good News. Pastor Herman's special mission was to minister to the tiniest, most out-of-the-way, pastorless congregations. Traipsing over hill and dale, Laszlo and Pastor Herman got to know virtually every part of the country. Peasant life mesmerized the young, impressionable Laszlo.

Laszlo visited scores of villages and hamlets with Pastor Herman, but his favorite place was undoubtedly Szentmarton. The village was the birthplace of Erzsebet and became Laszlo's home away from home. He spent many happy summers and holidays there with his grandparents. He played with the barefoot village kids in the dusty dirt streets and along the banks of the Somesul River. Laszlo often earned his keep by tending the cows in Szentmarton's lush pastures. On Easter visits he plowed the fields. At Christmas he pruned in the vine-yards. It was pure magic.

To Laszlo, Szentmarton seemed like one big, happy family. Laszlo was one of its sons. He knew everyone and everyone knew him. Most of the villagers were Reformed. The village had a rich spiritual life that was fully integrated with everyday life. The faithful worked, worshiped, played and prayed together throughout the week. Szentmarton became for Laszlo a model Christian community, the spirit of which he would later try to instill in his urban congregations. On his first preaching visit to Szentmarton after his ordination, Laszlo addressed the assembled congregation. "My brethren," he began in customary style, "I left this congregation as a tender of cows and now return as a tender of souls." The church folk were delighted to have this "shepherd" back home in any capacity.

Laszlo's formal education began in September, 1959, when he nervously trekked to Cluj's School No. 3 for the first time in the playful company of his older brothers and sisters. Before the war, the school had been the Reformed Church's elite High School for Girls. But in 1948 the new Communist authorities decreed the confiscation of church schools and placed them under state control. Transylvania's church schools once formed the backbone of the country's educational system. By the time Laszlo started school, they had ceased to exist.

For good measure, the Romanian regime also banned religious instruction in the newly nationalized schools. Atheistic Marxism-Leninism replaced Christianity in the curriculum. Virtually all children, Laszlo included, had to join the Communist youth organization, the Pioneers.

Publicly professing Christian teachers were often thrown out of their jobs. Such anti-religious measures were a part of the Communist government's plan to weaken the influence of the church on the future generation and to make the church socially irrelevant. Church schools and religious instruction were seen as subversive tools of Western "imperialism" and the old social order. But all the Communist Party's anti-religious propaganda was wasted on Laszlo. The living, vibrant faith of his parents, Pastor Herman and the country folk of Szentmarton had a far greater influence on Laszlo's developing mind.

Laszlo was a good student and, on the whole, liked school. He was accustomed to getting straight As during his early years. Laszlo's diligence waned somewhat in his teens, but he remained one of the best students in his class. His good grades and strong character earned him a place in a high school for college-bound students. This was no mean feat. First of all, very few students went on to college in Romania. Second, the authorities systematically discriminated against the children of pastors, especially Hungarians, in the selection process. Some Hungarian parents were willing to register their children under Romanianized first names or to pay bribes to pave the way for the educational advancement of their children. Such methods were incompatible with the principles of Istvan and Erzsebet. Laszlo and all his brothers and sisters won places in good high schools, and later colleges, through their own achievement.

Laszlo was most fond of literature, languages and philosophy. But good physics and math teachers sparked an interest in Laszlo for these subjects, too. Laszlo loved history, but not as taught in school. History lessons and textbooks were full of Communist propaganda and anti-Hungarian bias. Laszlo was lucky to attend a school in which the language of instruction was his mother tongue. The Romanian Communist authorities seemed to be determined by hook or by crook to eliminate the use of Hungarian in the schools. They aimed to assimilate the Hungarians into the Romanian nationality by cutting back opportunities for study in the mother tongue of the national minorities, especially in the countryside.

As Laszlo's high school days were drawing to a close, he was unsure about his future direction. His decision would be his alone. Istvan and Erzsebet allowed the children as they grew older to make important decisions for themselves. Laszlo encountered no pressure, subtle or otherwise, from his parents about his choice of a career. His older brothers and sisters had become doctors, teachers and engineers. But Laszlo was independent-minded.

He tinkered with the romantic idea of becoming a poet. After all, he had a flair for writing, and in Transylvania poets have traditionally been honored for articulating and preserving the spiritual and cultural traditions of the people. But under the difficult circumstances of the day, Laszlo decided that a more practical form of service would be more appropriate. He was interested in becoming a teacher and was sure he would do the job well. But in the end it was the example of his father and Pastors Herman and Dezso that tipped the balance in the direction of the ministry. He chose to follow in the footsteps of his father and grandfathers. In the fall of 1971, Laszlo enrolled in the Protestant Seminary in Cluj.

FOUR

The Making of
a Pastor

Laszlo's life really began in seminary, he says. Till then it had been rather conventional. The seminary was a once-august institution, founded in 1568 as the Reformation took root in Transylvania. The present buildings, just around the corner from the Tokes home, dated back to 1893–5. It was a world-renowned center of learning for Transylvania's Calvinists. In 1945 it became officially known as the United Protestant Theological Institute, when it started taking Hungarian-speaking Lutheran and Unitarian students.

By the time Laszlo began his studies, the seminary was a dismal shadow of its former glory. Some of the finest teachers had been removed for political reasons. Often those taking their place were mediocre. The Stalinist era in Romania had promoted many nonentities to positions of power in all sections of society. Some of the professors had only a rudimentary grasp of the subjects they were supposed to teach. The seminary was not altogether void of intelligent, conscientious professors. But by and large they had been cut off from academic and social developments in the outside world by the Romanian police state. The Communist authorities knew that by lowering the standards at the seminary they could lower the standard of pastors for generations to come. Standards had plummeted at the finest institution of the Reformed Church. Even the buildings, once kept so finely, began to lose their splendor.

When Laszlo began the four-year course, the name Tokes was already well known at the Protestant Seminary. Istvan was known by all the professors there. Laszlo soon won a reputation as a highly intelligent but rather doctrinaire student. Some of his fellow students thought he had many fixed ideas that he had unquestioningly accepted from his father, his grandfathers, Pastor Dezso and other members of the older generation of clergymen.

The atmosphere of the seminary was arid and stuffy, but Laszlo did not lack stimulation for long. It came not as much from the professors as from some of his fellow students—Janos Molnar in particular. It was a fateful day indeed when Laszlo first met the short, ginger-haired Janos in 1971. Janos was somewhat different from the other students. He had not gone to seminary straight from high school. His original calling had been as an artist. Janos had studied art for several years before he had to give up on doctor's orders. The fumes from paints and cleaning fluids were ruining his eyes.

Janos, in his second year at the seminary when Laszlo

arrived, was instrumental in changing the atmosphere. The final-year students were more traditional: quiet, studious and unambitious. They had set their sights low. Janos and several other students entering the seminary in the early 1970s were different. They were more idealistic and eager to break out of the restraining influences of the past. They had been inspired by the ideals of the student movements that swept the Western world in 1968—ideals that took several years to penetrate the barriers of Ceausescu's police state. The fresh influx of seminarians was less fearful in challenging the old, conformist order than the older group.

The Molnar Circle

Janos Molnar and his circle of friends—Laci Nagy, Janos Vitez and Sandor Biro—knew other student leaders at Cluj University. The university students had formed a free association, independent from the official, government-controlled student body. They also started their own independent newspaper. But they were obstructed by the authorities at every turn. Through Janos the university students learned that the seminary was less tightly controlled by the Securitate than the university. The Communist authorities then thought of the seminary as a sleepy, unthreatening place that merited no special attention. After all, there had been no serious trouble there for many years. This band of university and seminary students agreed to try to make the Protestant Seminary a center for Cluj's embryonic student movement.

Laszlo was torn in two directions. He was attracted to the excitement and daring of Janos Molnar. He felt really free for the first time in his life in the company of Molnar's circle. His mind was stimulated. He felt at home in this close-knit community, which did not respect the taboos of the Communist regime. But the influence of his father pulled him the other way. Istvan was a sharp critical thinker himself and wished to bring about badly needed reform in the Church. But Istvan was then wary of involvement in the affairs of the world outside the Church—especially in anything that smacked of political opposition. He feared for the welfare of his son. The kinds of things Molnar was involved in were extremely dangerous in Ceausescu's Romania. Violent repression in Romania was now at a low point. But Istvan could well remember little more than ten years earlier, when scores of Reformed pastors were imprisoned in a government crackdown on the Hungarian community. His strongly worded advice to Laszlo was to stay clear of Molnar and company!

The young, impressionable Laszlo could not resist the temptation. The thought of a conventional life depressed him. All around he could see those who would not dare to be different. He was not impressed. Life is more than studying, earning a living and dying, he thought. Laszlo gravitated closer and closer to his friend, eventually becoming a trusted member of Molnar's inner circle of confidants.

The Molnar circle daringly formed an independent association of students and started their own newspaper. They called it "?"—Question Mark—and compiled it in secret. They took their handwritten text to the deputy dean to ask his permission to circulate it officially. The deputy dean was taken aback by this organization of students. This was the first he had heard of it. His spies had failed to inform him of it. The deputy dean did not know what to do. "This is very useful and correct," he told them, "but you should ask the dean." He was trying to shuffle responsibility for the decision upward. He took the manuscript to his boss immediately. After an hour he emerged from the dean's office. "Destroy the manuscript and forget all about it!" he ordered.

The Molnar circle also undertook a sociological survey among the youth regarding their attitudes toward religion. This was a taboo subject in Communist Romania. They were unaware of any previous attempt to conduct such a survey in the country. They sought professional help from the staff of a local sociological journal in preparing the questionnaire. The questions were rather direct and sensitive. They asked about church problems, politics and culture. Many people refused to answer them, fearing the consequences of their opinions becoming known to the authorities. However, the survey was finally finished, giving them at least an approximate idea of the views of young people.

The results of the survey were presented to one of the more open-minded professors at the seminary. Molnar and his friends hoped to have the results published. The professor found their work fascinating. But only a small part of the survey was ever published. The rest was burnt in the stove of the professor's room.

Another aim of the Molnar circle was to get Hungarian language and literature on the syllabus. All theological instruction at the seminary was in Hungarian, but the teaching of Hungarian literature was forbidden by the state. Eager to weaken the linguistic bulwark of the Hungarian nation, the authorities permitted only the teaching of Romanian literature at the Protestant Seminary. Laszlo and his friends who had attended Hungarian schools were shocked to find that some of the Hungarian seminary students who graduated from Romanian schools had a hard time reading and writing in their mother tongue.

While Laszlo was at seminary, Ceausescu was intensifying the Communists' policy of assimilating Romania's minorities and crushing their separate identities. Hungarians and Germans, as well as the smaller communities of Serbians and Ukrainians, were the victims of this new policy. Schools, newspapers, radio: all were restricted in every language except Romanian. Many Hungarian schools were turned "bilingual," and Romanian started to take over. Romanians were brought in to teach in Hungarian areas, while Hungarian teachers were offered jobs only in Romanian areas. Severe restrictions were imposed on the numbers studying Hungarian at the universities. Hungarian newspapers became mere shadows of their Romanian counterparts, containing many articles translated from the Romanian press. Hungarian theaters had to produce Romanian plays in Hungarian translation.

When Laszlo visited his beloved Szentmarton, he could see the decline in Hungarian village life. Young Hungarians had left for the towns, leaving only the elderly behind. Romanians had been brought in by the government from regions outside Transylvania. The policy of transferring masses of Romanians from Wallachia and Moldavia to Transylvania affected Hungarian towns and villages alike. This social engineering in Szentmarton symbolized for Laszlo the loss of Hungarian identity. He felt this loss deeply.

The Molnar circle failed in its attempt to start Hungarian literature classes as a part of the seminary's official curriculum. But if it could not be done in the classroom, then Laszlo and his colleagues would do it outside. Laszlo became president of the Hungarian cultural group at the seminary. About 180 students participated. Many were from the university. Laszlo made arrangements for Cluj's leading literary figures to speak to the group.

Each Thursday evening, Laszlo brought fellow students back to his parents' apartment. They gathered in the stately living room, surrounded by pictures and sculptures. There they recited Hungarian poetry and talked about their favorite writers. Laszlo's mother Erzsebet was one of the keenest participants. She was in her element when sharing her fondness for poetry with Laszlo and his companions. The lovers of literature talked and performed till late at night. At about eleven o'clock, Istvan would leave his books and papers in his study and join them. He would invite them to have a glass of wine while he addressed these select members of the Reformed Church's new generation. The wine would often get warm in their glasses as he spoke at length of the need for a spiritual revolution in the Church. He spoke with passion as his young audience listened attentively.

Laszlo and the Molnar circle tried to change the petty regulations that governed their lives at the seminary. The rules were so strict that even a Catholic monastery would have been proud of them, Molnar recalls. Students had to be in by ten o'clock at night. If they arrived back later, they had to sign a book, declaring where they had been and giving the names of two eyewitnesses who could confirm it. The Molnar circle wanted to have a freely elected student council, but the dean firmly resisted any attempts to reform the seminary. The professors always blamed the state authorities for the restrictions, hinting darkly that there was pressure on them and that the state preferred the setup as it was. Relations between the younger students and the teaching staff became tense.

The authorities—both the Securitate and the seminary officials—were very unhappy about all the commotion made by the Molnar circle. They tried to isolate the theological students as much as possible from the university students. They feared the free exchange of ideas, not knowing where that would lead. The Securitate feared the political implications of the Molnar circle's activity. The more traditional professors thought it was enough for seminarians to study the Bible and theological texts. They wanted the seminary to return to the quiet backwater it was before the arrival of Janos Molnar, Laszlo Tokes and friends. But these energetic students were determined not to be isolated from the rest of society. They continued to hold open discussion groups with students from the university and were soon playing football with students from Cluj's Orthodox seminary.

The student unrest came to a head in 1972, the year after Laszlo started his studies. The authorities feared the situation was getting out of hand. Seventeen students were suspended, some for one or two months, others for a year. Janos—by now in his third year—was suspended for a year and banished from Cluj to prevent him from having further contact with his erstwhile colleagues. Laci Nagy was spared the harshest punishment, probably because his father was the bishop. He was transferred for a year from Cluj to the German Lutheran seminary in Sibiu. Laszlo, too, escaped relatively unscathed, perhaps because of Istvan's growing influence in church life.

During Janos's one-year absence, a whole mythology about him grew up. He became larger than life in the minds of the students. He returned the next year to a hero's welcome. The authorities had badly miscalculated. His influence was now greater than ever. The new spirit continued among the students.

Not all the students were sympathetic to Laszlo and the Molnar circle. The Securitate had informers within their ranks. Some had been agents before they began their studies, others were recruited on entrance or later. This bred an atmosphere of mistrust and suspicion among the students. You could never be sure when a careless remark might get back to the Securitate and be dredged up to haunt you weeks, months, or even years later. The Securitate was delighted at the demoralization it was causing.

Revival in the Church

Notwithstanding the dangers and obstacles, Laszlo and his friends were intent on bringing about a revival in the Church they had dedicated their lives to. The Church, which the Communists had brought to its knees, needed to be reinvigorated. Laszlo and his friends saw no hope in the present generation of Church leaders who had been set up by the Communists: the Bishop of Cluj, Gyula Nagy, and the Bishop of Oradea, Laszlo Papp.

The years of Romanian Stalinism had seen the Communist state tighten its grip on every church in the country. The Orthodox Church—the biggest church in the country—had come completely under the control of the state. Bishops had been removed from office, as well as hundreds of priests. New, pliable priests were promoted by the government to run the Church under close supervision. The Eastern-rite Catholic Church, which proclaimed allegiance to the Vatican, was brutally suppressed with the help of the Orthodox hierarchy. The Roman Catholics were severely restricted in their activities, as were the Lutherans and other Protestants. Many clergymen and laypeople of all churches were sent to prison, where many died.

New laws on religion were introduced in 1948 by the Communist-dominated government, and in 1950 the state forced the hard-pressed leaders of the Reformed Church to sign an unfavorable agreement. The state now claimed the right to interfere in every Church activity. No clergyman could be ordained or appointed without government approval, no church could be opened, buildings could not even be painted, without express permission. Concessions from the state to the Church were granted as rewards for good political behavior.

The government exercised its control overtly through the Department of Religious Affairs in Bucharest. The department also had local representatives throughout the country. Covertly, the ever-present Securitate also played a key role. No institution in Romania escaped its scrutiny. As in most Communist countries, the Department of Religious Affairs had to approve all church activities. It even decided what groups constituted a legal church. Unless a church was recognized by the state, all activities were regarded as illegal. Romania was proud of telling the world it had fourteen recognized denominations. But recognition was symptomatic of the totalitarian regime's desire to control every church's every activity.

Laszlo and the Molnar circle understood the Communists' methods of control. They could see the disastrous consequences all around them. They devised an astonishing plan to reverse this trend. Calculating coolly, they aimed to beat the Communists at their own game. They aimed to infiltrate themselves slowly and quietly into positions of authority until they gained control of the whole Church. In Communist Romania this was a dangerous game to play. The Communists knew how dangerous conspiracies were.

The conspirators went on seemingly innocuous trips into the hills, far from everywhere. What could be more harmless than a group of fellow students off for a walking holiday in the countryside? They sat down in the spectacular scenery and devised a concrete plan. They worked out which informer was to be removed from what post. They calculated how this could be achieved. During the summer holidays, the Molnar circle met frequently, visiting each other in their own towns and villages. Almost every weekend in spring and autumn, they were off on their trips. Thus the bonds of friendship and trust strengthened.

Living at home, although only two minutes from the

seminary, Laszlo felt slightly cut off from his fellow students. In the middle of his course he decided to move in and share fully in seminary life. Only in this way could he have maximum influence. The last two years—including his final year, when he was student president—he spent in close quarters with his fellow students. Laszlo became one of the most committed and daring members of the Molnar circle, drawing up plans for a dangerous counterespionage operation within the Securitate.

But Laszlo was careful to listen to his friends who shrank from such a potentially deadly adventure. Over the years Laszlo matured. He was serious and articulate. He spoke in slow but carefully composed sentences. His thoughts were clear and precise. He could penetrate to the heart of any subject. His fellow students were often convinced by his reasoning. But Laszlo respected their opinions as well.

Laszlo and his fellow conspirators for renewal concocted a carefully thought-out plan. They selected one deanery to mount their takeover bid. Their plan would be most likely to succeed in one of the smallest, so they chose the deanery centered in Brasov (in Hungarian, Brasso). This had relatively few congregations, though it was the largest in terms of area, encompassing all of Romania outside Transylvania. Because the congregations in Brasov deanery tended to be small, few pastors wanted to work there. Thus the Molnar circle figured the turnover of pastors would be high. Within five or six years they could control the deanery. They divided the congregations among themselves and requested appointments there. Laszlo chose the town of Brasov for himself. They were attempting to rebuild a vigorous, independent church from the grass roots up.

During Laszlo's final year, the authorities again tried to clamp down on the activities and influence of the Molnar circle. Students of other colleges in Cluj were forbidden to enter the seminary building. The dean wanted to abolish the literary circle, which Janos led. In the spring of 1975, the Securitate ordered all the students to come for individual talks. Janos was hauled in. "We know you are intelligent and well-educated," the officer told him in Hungarian. "It is your patriotic duty to give the Securitate information about the behavior, habits and thoughts of your fellow students." Janos refused. The man then took a copy of a sermon Janos had given to the students in the auditorium. There were only two copies of the speech—Janos had one and had given the other to his professor. Now it was here in the Securitate man's hands. "You know you could be sent to prison for three or five years for this," he warned.

Laszlo was not so harshly treated during his interrogation. Istvan had recently become a professor at the seminary and deputy bishop. Perhaps this was the cause of Laszlo's good fortune. Laszlo refused all forms of cooperation, as did many of the students. But the Securitate was achieving one of its aims—it was spreading mistrust among the students. Soon afterward, they established a permanent office within the seminary. A Securitate officer openly roamed the building in uniform. One of the professors had to be turned out of his office to make room for him.

Laszlo completed his studies at the seminary in 1975. The portraits of those graduating were eventually added to the old-fashioned montages of teachers and students that adorn the seminary's dingy staircase. Laszlo knew he would miss the intimate camaraderie of the Molnar circle. But on the whole he was pleased to be leaving the seminary behind, with its loathsome, obstructive atmosphere. Its rigid, fossilized spirit was frustrating and oppressive. The spying and collaboration with the authorities was demoralizing. By the time he left, the conflicts with the authorities were getting worse. Within those few years Laszlo had turned into a radical, determined to oppose those who were trying to destroy the Church. His work was soon to begin.

First Steps

Laszlo's wish came true. He was appointed to serve as assistant pastor in Brasov—a large town where Germans, Romanians and Hungarians are all represented in large numbers. Others in the Molnar circle were also placed in the Brasov deanery. Laci Nagy went to Galati—refusing his father's wish for him to stay in Cluj. Another went to Bacau. Karoly Nagy was appointed to the church in the capital, Bucharest. The seminary conspirators set about fulfilling their aim: the renewal of the Reformed Church. Their first task was to revive declining congregations.

Laszlo was happy to be in Brasov. This was what he had prepared long and hard for: the ministry. Laszlo loved the renewed contact with ordinary church members. The people of the Brasov congregation welcomed him with open arms.

The Brasov church had a good pastor who was active in youth work. Laszlo joined in enthusiastically, organizing a lecture and discussion group for college students. More and more young people began to attend church. Once a week he had to travel to the pastorless village of Zernesti to hold services. At last the work was beginning, and it was growing beautifully. Laszlo moved cautiously but steadily toward his goal, wishing to avoid needless controversy.

However, Laszlo had not been in Brasov long when he received an unexpected visitor. It was the Securitate official responsible for church affairs back in Cluj. He brought with him a fat file full of documents gathered during Laszlo's days at the seminary. The official calmly informed him he was viewed as a nationalist and a mystic. The government had its eye on him, too. Nothing escaped its view.

Things began to go wrong for Laszlo. He got wind of rumors about his private life. The authorities refused to give him a passport. The last time he had traveled abroad was nearly ten years earlier, when he was fourteen. Laszlo had been labeled as a political criminal. He was being closely monitored by the Securitate's Office for the Investigation of Nationalists, Fascists and Hungarian Irredentists. Among its duties was to try to compromise Hungarian pastors and to destroy the reputations of conscientious clergy through rumor and innuendo.

FIVE

A Bittersweet Ministry

After two years in Brasov, Laszlo took up an assistant pastorate in the town of Dej. He was glad to be back on home turf, close to both friends and family in Cluj and Szentmarton. He arrived in 1977 as second in command to Pastor Jozsef Laposi. The town of 50,000 people—mostly Romanians—had about 5,000 Reformed inhabitants. About 500 of them came regularly to the one Reformed church—a graceful fifteenth-century Gothic building with a tall spire that dominated the old town.

Laszlo lived in a single room in a one-story house down a side street next to the church. The windows looked out onto the road, but the entrance was around the back, in the yard. A path led through the overgrown yard past wooden barns. The room was plain, almost monastic, with simple whitewashed walls. A large tiled stove stood near the door. The bathroom was a curtained-off area in the corner on the other side of the door. The room was small but pleasant and airy, especially in summer with the breezes drifting in through the open door. Laszlo's neighbor on the street was the pastor, who occupied the next house, with its spacious rooms and well-kept garden. It was here, with its large desk, portraits on the walls, and shabby carpet, that the church office was situated.

This was one of the happiest periods of Laszlo's life. He had much work to do and threw himself into it with gusto. The outgoing Laszlo quickly made friends: a doctor, a bookseller, a teacher. All sorts of people came and went from Laszlo's room.

Their common interest was Hungarian literature, art and music. Laszlo's social circle became something of an unofficial cultural association. They wanted to revive national traditions that were becoming extinct in Ceausescu's Romania.

Laszlo and his companions introduced their circle to the people of Dej with a special evening in honor of the celebrated Hungarian poet Endre Ady in 1977. News of the evening traveled far and wide. There followed a flowering of Hungarian culture within the town.

Laszlo and his friends became famous—or notorious— through this Ady evening. The authorities allowed it to go ahead, but they immediately took note of Laszlo and his friends. They were now troublemakers to be watched. They went on to form a folk dance club. They established classes, gathered in the children, set up nurseries and organized folk music evenings. Fiddlers, flautists and guitar players came to their dance sessions from Cluj, forty miles away. Dej had been a cultural desert, both for Hungarians and Romanians. Now Hungarian culture was experiencing a rebirth.

In what was perhaps their most ambitious project, they founded what they called a "free university"—a grandiose name for the small study group, but a sign of their ambition. This met in Laszlo's apartment. In Ceausescu's Romania—where everything, especially education, came under close government supervision—this was a daring step. They had a network of scholars, actors and cultural specialists who were willing to give classes.

The young people warmed to their energetic new pastor. They squeezed into Laszlo's single room, where they spent hours talking, discussing and arguing. Only about thirty people could cram into the small room, some sitting on the bed, others perched on the edge of Laszlo's desk.

Laszlo believed in participation. His Bible classes were far from the rigid, old-fashioned lectures, where the pastor did all the talking and the students just listened. When the high school pupils gathered around Laszlo, they had to be prepared to study and participate. Laszlo made them do much of the talking. Lively discussion ensued, which was not confined to strictly religious topics. The gatherings in his cramped room were true exchanges of ideas.

Ever conscious of their history, they named the Bible study group after Lajos Medgyes, a former pastor of the Dej congregation. Medgyes gained fame for his military exploits in the Hungarian War of Independence in 1849 and for his poetry. Pastor Medgyes was not typical of the Hungarians of his day. While a good Hungarian patriot, he promoted reconciliation with the Romanians. He recognized that Transylvania belonged to ethnic Romanians as well as Hungarians. Laszlo considered him a good example for the Hungarians of Transylvania.

But Laszlo didn't just stay at home waiting for people to call. He was always out and about in the town. And he was eager to involve the community in the life of the church. Christmas was a time to reach out to the people. He adopted a Catholic custom: a midnight service on Christmas Eve. He gathered the young people and went from house to house, singing carols. With Laszlo's strong voice leading the singing, they spent all night visiting the faithful. This special celebration started in 1982 and continued for four years, even after Laszlo had gone, until it was stopped on orders from the Securitate after Christmas, 1985.

It was not just the young people who were attracted to Laszlo: ordinary members of the church started asking for him to perform baptisms and weddings instead of the pastor. In 1983, the council of elders elected Laszlo as their permanent assistant pastor. This was important to Laszlo later on as a sign of their spontaneous regard for him. This also meant that he was now no longer subject to the bishop but directly to the elders' council.

To Laszlo, the most important thing about this period was that it taught him to be reflective. He and his co-workers had a bold plan: from cradle to grave they would have contact with everyone. Laszlo naturally had an important role in this: as pastor it was his job to care for his flock. But he did not look only to his own flock. Catholic and Reformed, teacher and priest—all were welcomed.

One Step Ahead

Laszlo's group was viewed with real suspicion. The authorities—the school, the Dej Securitate—conspired to obstruct its activities. Laszlo's pastor, Jozsef Laposi, was concerned that it was drawing too much attention and disturbing the quiet life of the church. As opposition mounted, Laszlo and his friends drew their support from the enthusiasm of the Hungarian community. Every week the Bible study circle, which had an English language section, met. The members seized every opportunity to do something different. This kept them one step ahead of the authorities, who were never sure how to react.

After a while, there was opposition to everything Laszlo and his friends did. Laszlo had a plan to restore the neglected graves in Dej's Hungarian cemetery. The Romanian authorities were notorious for desecrating Hungarian graves. By so doing, they hoped to remove historical evidence of the Hungarian presence in the country. He and his friends started to list the graves and tidy up the graveyard. The authorities soon told them to stop. Pressure came indirectly—the authorities put pressure on Laszlo via the council of elders.

It was Laszlo's theatrical activities that first led him into serious conflict with the authorities. He and his friends put together a program of verse under the title "Past and Future." There was nothing objectionable in it on ideological grounds, even to the Communists. Both Romanian and Hungarian poets were included. But the authorities demanded major changes. In the first part, they determined, no more than 40 percent should be in Hungarian. In the second, everything had to be performed in

Romanian. Laszlo and his friends were forced to comply.

The local authorities initiated a well-thought-out campaign against Laszlo and his circle, intending to force Laszlo out of the theatrical group. The potentially dynamic combination of religion and living culture seemed dangerous. Their campaign lasted many months. Laszlo's friends were regularly hauled in for questioning. The interrogators accused Laszlo of corrupting the youth and undermining socialist culture—grave offenses in Communist Romania. But they kept their hands off Laszlo. Their tactic was to throw seeds of resentment and suspicion into the group. "Why does the Securitate harass me and not our leaders, like Laszlo?" some asked. "Perhaps he is a cunning Securitate informer himself!" answered others. But most did not doubt Laszlo's integrity. Finally, his heart torn by the intimidation of his friends, Laszlo decided to yield. He did not want to land his friends in further trouble and further endanger their good work. He withdrew from the group.

Laszlo had no choice but to keep his distance. Everywhere walls had ears. Everything was reported back. Then informers got to work on the Bible circle. In the end, this destroyed it. The Communist regime had a vast network of spies. Some were paid, others were voluntary, hoping for a favor in return for denouncing their neighbors. One of Ceausescu's former security chiefs, Ion Pacepa, claims that one in four or five Romanians was a paid informer.

Laszlo, for one, believes this to be something of an exaggeration. But spies abounded. Plenty of informers were on hand to keep the Securitate informed about Laszlo's activities.

The other leader of the cultural circle, a teacher named Jolan Kalapati, suffered too. She was active in both the drama and the folk dance groups. In 1983 she was banished from Dej and sent to the distant town of Huedin.

Getting Nowhere

Istvan Tokes was growing despondent. By nature he was an optimist. But he was now beginning to think the prospect for reform in the Reformed Church might be hopeless. Istvan had been convinced that renewal could be achieved by working through the institutions and structures of the Church. After all, they had served the Reformed Church very well for centuries. But those hallowed institutions and structures were being steadily eroded by the state and its puppets, Bishops Nagy and Papp. Since becoming deputy bishop in the early 1970s, Istvan had been doing battle behind the scenes with Bishop Nagy. But he was getting nowhere.

Church life was reaching a depressing point, Istvan thought. Although the Church claimed to have 700,000 members, active participation in church life was much less. Many ministers, around whom most church life revolved, behaved more like bureaucrats. They just performed the rites of passage. Services did not excite ordinary people. New methods were needed: Bible classes for different age groups, choirs, youth singing groups, home prayers and family visits.

Everything hinged on the pastor. Where he was active and combined both old and new community activities, church life was bustling. But life was not easy for such pastors. They faced opposition from both church and state.

Istvan laid the blame for the sorry state of the Church squarely at the door of the two bishops. They ruled as autocrats. If the Church constitution stood in the way of meeting objectives, they simply ignored it. Both bishops meekly accepted all the government's restrictions. Severe limits on the numbers that could enter the seminaries affected church life drastically. Many churches, especially in country areas, remained without a pastor. The bishops did nothing to try to remedy the situation.

At times the bishops seemed almost dedicated to wiping out their own Church. This was particularly true of Papp, who lacked the sophistication to cover his tracks when performing dirty deeds. Both bishops sabotaged attempts to revive church activity. They favored pastors who confined their activity to carrying out baptisms, weddings and funerals. Pastors taking active steps to revive the faith were routinely punished by transferral and other methods.

At first Istvan thought that Bishop Nagy was less in the pocket of the regime than Papp. But as the conflict deepened, Istvan was gradually beginning to change his view of Nagy. Papp's unpleasantness was something apparent to all. He made no attempt to hide it. Nagy, on the other hand, seemed reasonable on the surface. Bishop Nagy began to move against Istvan in 1979, soon after Istvan had tried to goad the synod into curbing the bishops' power. Nagy managed to halt all discussion of Istvan's proposal. From that day on, Istvan believes, Nagy schemed to remove him from his posts.

By now, Istvan was deputy bishop, professor in the seminary and an editor of the Church's theological jour-

nal, *Reformed Review*. In 1983, Bishop Nagy finally succeeded. Istvan's "revolutionary" ideas—returning to the
historic, constitutional principles of his Calvinist Church
—were removed from the Church's agenda.

Publishing Problems

Laszlo always tried to act as openly as he could, and he
believed in doing so within the country. Even under
Ceausescu it was possible to smuggle out messages and
have them broadcast back to Romania over foreign radio.
But Laszlo was reluctant to make use of foreign forums.
He always tried to find an audience first of all in his own
church and in his native land. He chose what he regarded
as legitimate ways of putting forward his views, so that
the authorities could not quibble about the methods he
had used.

Laszlo wrote to Bishop Nagy to complain that there
were not enough church calendars published to give out
to all those requiring them. The bishop asked him why he
was complaining.

As the government restricted the production and import of Hungarian religious books, the shortage of hymnbooks worsened. Laszlo also wrote about this, risking the
immediate wrath of the state by signing the memos with
his own name. He believed in doing as much as was legally possible. He was not cowed into submission like so
many of his compatriots.

The shortage of Hungarian books was made worse toward the end of the 1970s, when the government started
restricting the importing of books from Hungary. Even

newspapers and periodicals were banned. It was impossible to import Bibles and religious books. Since virtually none were produced within Romania—either in Romanian or Hungarian—the shortage soon became acute.

Most of the available religious books dated from before the war. Some were even from the last century. If members of the church had Bibles or hymnbooks, they were usually old and tatty through much use. The churches had no books to give out at each service.

But as the Reformed bishops traveled the world on behalf of the government, they denied there was a shortage. Laszlo Papp declared at international conferences that there were plenty of Bibles. So a pastor, Gyula Sogor of Cimpa Turzii, went to Papp to collect fifty copies for his congregation. Papp could not give him even one copy. In 1980, the same pastor was brought a few boxes of Hungarian Bibles by a Dutch tour group, which had managed to smuggle them through the border. But the Bibles were confiscated by the Securitate. Pastor Sogor was subjected to a five-hour interrogation. If he had been caught distributing them, he would have been sentenced to between one and five years in prison.

The worst case allegedly happened with a consignment of Hungarian Bibles. In 1972 and 1981 the World Alliance of Reformed Churches sent two shipments, of 10,000 copies each, to the Reformed Church in Romania. It is said that fewer than 200 copies were delivered to the churches, the rest being pulped by the government into toilet paper. Sitting on a train one day, a Romanian worker from a paper factory in Braila told Janos Molnar quite by chance about the pulping. The worker said that Bibles were also being pulped in other paper factories in southern Romania. Some of the workers, believers themselves, were so horrified that they stole copies to send abroad. At press conferences in the United States, strips of alleged toilet paper with Bible words visible were displayed.

The available evidence strongly suggests that the Ceausescu regime did pulp Bibles sent from the West. But whether they were the copies sent by the World Alliance of Reformed Churches or Bibles confiscated from smugglers is unclear. When the storm broke in the West in 1985, Bishop Papp was forced to issue a denial of the story. He maintained that the WARC Bibles were distributed in the two church districts through the deaneries. He expressed his "astonishment and repulsion" at the allegations that the Bibles had been turned into toilet paper.

Anonymous Articles

Laszlo did not succeed in raising the quota of students entering theological college. Nor did he succeed in getting the ban on the publishing and importing of Hungarian hymnbooks lifted. The authorities took more and more measures to harass him and restrict his freedom of action. He was put under closer surveillance. Storm clouds began to gather.

As surveillance tightened, he decided to break his pattern, publishing a series of anonymous articles. Everywhere in the Eastern bloc, unoffical publications were launched, challenging the state's monopoly on published opinion. Using typewriters and carbon paper or homemade duplicating machines, *samizdat* was born. In spite of universal opposition from Communist governments throughout the region, the number of publications mushroomed. Religious, political, philosophical, even musical works banned officially were published and circulated. Many authors and private publishers were sent to prison and some publications were short-lived. But writers and publishers persisted.

Romania was different, though. It was a police state in a way that recalled Nazi Germany or Stalinist Russia. Hard-line Communism and a strong and brutal leader, combined with an all-seeing security police, prevented dissident activity from taking place. Dissent was soon crushed. Those who spoke out were usually soon silenced.

In 1981—much later than in other Communist countries—a group of Hungarians in Romania got together to begin an independent opposition journal. They called it *Counterpoints* (*Ellenpontok,* in Hungarian). It was the first major *samizdat* periodical in Romania. Its three editors were Geza Szocs, Attila Ara-Kovacs and Karoly Toth.

Laszlo was never in the inner circle, but the editors were looking for someone to write about the Reformed Church. They initially wanted to approach Laci Nagy but decided he would probably be too afraid. Janos Molnar suggested asking Laszlo, who agreed to contribute articles to the journal on a confidential basis. It had to be compiled and produced in such secrecy that even Laszlo did not know exactly who received his articles. But they began to appear.

The editors had contact with dissidents in Poland and Hungary, where there was a longer tradition of underground publishing. In Poland, publications ranged from cultural to Catholic to ecological to anarchist. A bewildering array of magazines, journals, even books came off the secret presses. From their Polish colleagues, the editors learned the primitive techniques of duplicating.

The first issue—published in Oradea in December, 1981—had a pressrun of less than 100 copies, though this was increased by enthusiastic readers making further copies at home in secret. In spite of the risks, the number of readers gradually increased. People begged and borrowed copies from friends. It was a small start in the revival of independent, uncensored thought in Transylvania.

By the end of 1982, the authorities were close on the editors' tail. Attila Ara-Kovacs was arrested in November and held for three weeks. During his interrogation, the Securitate seemed particularly interested in his contacts with Laszlo.

Also arrested in November was twenty-eight-year-old Sandor Dienes from Satu Mare in the north of the country. He was lining up for food when the police swooped in. Interrogated during the winter months, he was sentenced in February to two years imprisonment. He was not even allowed to attend his own trial. Sandor had already been in trouble while studying at the Cluj seminary in 1978.

The arrests started in Oradea, but arrests and searches followed in Tirgu Mures, Cluj and elsewhere. The Securitate knocked on Janos Molnar's door on January 6, 1983. During a house search, the Securitate found a poem that had been published anonymously in the first issue of *Counterpoints,* back in 1981. Janos did not deny he had written it. Besides his literary articles, Janos had also contributed critical articles on the government-controlled church press in Romania.

Attila was freed from prison in December, but until the following May he was kept under house arrest in his apartment in Oradea. He was determined to continue his secret publishing work. From his house arrest, Attila founded the Hungarian Press of Transylvania. This was to be an independent news service giving reliable information on the true situation of the Hungarians in Romania.

Attila organized a network of friends in secret from his third-floor apartment. The Securitate watched the door of his building but did not conduct surveillance inside. A Romanian friend who lived on the fifth floor, a doctor by profession, smuggled messages out to his friends.

Counterpoints continued into 1983. Nine issues were published before the authorities succeeded in stamping it out. Geza Szocs and Karoly Toth were both arrested that year. Attila was unwittingly saved from further repression by the American government. The Most Favored Nation trade concession, which Romania had first gained in 1975, was up for annual review. As always, the Romanian government was trying to polish up its human rights image just before the crucial vote. On May 25, Attila received a phone call in Oradea from the Securitate. He had just five hours to leave the country.

The Ceausescu regime was not content to punish just the writers and editors of *Counterpoints*. A crackdown began against all possible dissident activity. The Romanian government would have none of the dissent that had spread like cancer into its Eastern European neighbors. There was to be no Romanian Solidarity or Charter 77. The government imposed a new decree in early 1983. All typewriters in the country had to be registered with the police. People who were not considered suitable had theirs taken away or were not permitted to buy one. Once a year, the owners would have to present the police with a specimen of the typewriter's print face. In this way the Securitate could trace the origin of anonymously typed documents.

In retaliation for the journal and to prevent the growth of a new dissident generation, the government started restricting the numbers of students in the Cluj seminary. In the 1950s and '60s the average entry was more than fifty students per year. After the crackdown, the number was cut to below twenty. The total number of students fell from 162 in 1979 to 51 in 1985. In 1986 more than seventy candidates took the entrance examinations, but only eighteen were accepted for both Cluj and Sibiu together. At least 100 new pastors a year were needed to replace those retiring or dying.

The authorities also started cutting back severely on the numbers entering the Catholic seminary in Alba Iulia, the only Catholic Hungarian seminary in Romania. The Communist authorities only allowed between thirty and fifty new students each year, although Transylvania as a whole needed about 100 to maintain the number of priests. In 1984 this intake was cut further to thirty, with only fifteen the next year. The authorities were trying to strangle the churches.

The Securitate had been investigating Laszlo's involvement with *Counterpoints*. Suspecting he was the author of the articles on the Church, they concealed cameras outside the house and waited to catch him. Finally they got the photographs they wanted: he was snapped accepting copies of the journal from Geza Szocs. The picture was so clear that one could read the title of the journal.

The Authorities Act

Swift action followed. Laszlo's house was immediately searched. He was traveling by rail one day when Securitate officials hauled him off the train. They told him a burglary had taken place in his home. But when they got to his home, they started searching it for incriminating writings. They confiscated his papers. Laszlo was afraid they would beat him up. The Securitate were never shy about physically attacking their victims. But it seemed they were afraid of attacking a servant of the Lord. This time Laszlo avoided a brutal beating and major injuries. He escaped with only minor bruises on his face as the Securitate agents jostled him. They had not tried to break him physically—this time, at least.

Although Laszlo denied being involved in editing the journal, this sparked the Securitate's specific plans to have him removed from Dej. At that time, Laszlo wanted to focus his activity on strictly religious themes. He felt that by steering away from political involvement he could achieve more to revive the Church.

But his home continued to be searched. Laszlo always locked the door of his room with two keys. Every time he went out now, he put a sign on the locks so that he could see if they were tampered with. Now he had proof that the secret police were breaking in when he was away.

At the Securitate's instigation, the woman who lived in the room next to his complained that he was playing his radio too loud late at night and that she could not sleep. The woman was known to have relatives in the secret police. Harassment was being stepped up on all fronts.

Laszlo was hauled before Bishop Gyula Nagy for a disciplinary hearing—at Securitate instigation. They had already sent anonymous letters "proving" the accusations against him. But what were the accusations? Laszlo asked help from the well-known Hungarian journalist in Bucharest, Pal Bodor. A committee was set up. The result was a delay of a good half-year.

Laszlo was worried, though, since the regime had already set itself on the course of liquidating its enemies. There were many people who "disappeared." Hair-raising lies were being spread. In this light, it seemed trivial to try to make the authorities observe the legal niceties.

The church council, too, was put under strong Securitate pressure. They stood firm beside their popular pastor—right to the bitter end. Because of their loyalty, the proceedings had to be postponed many times. But the judgment had already been reached.

Twice members of the church wrote to Bishop Nagy to support Laszlo. Twice delegations went to his office in Cluj. Forty people went in the first delegation, but when they arrived they were told, "The bishop is not at home." The bishop had heard they were coming and was prepared. For two days the delegation stayed in the yard outside his office. "We will wait!" they said. They spoke loudly so that everyone in the church offices could hear. Finally Nagy allowed them inside. Before the bishop sat down, everyone had to write down his or her name and address. The bishop did not say why.

The list was later handed to the Securitate. They visited the house of every single member of the delegation. People were warned and threatened. "Your children will lose their jobs," some members of the group were told.

Laszlo did not want to cause people unnecessary trouble. He stopped visiting people—exactly what the Securitate wanted. But not everyone was cowed. One member of the church was asked how often Laszlo came to visit and why he came around so frequently. "He is a good friend," he told the Securitate. "If you have problems, you should sort them out with him directly." And he said to Laszlo that he would always be welcome in his home.

The case finally came before the Dej district church court. The judges were old, feeble and lacking in courage. They voted three to two to order Laszlo's transfer. When one of the judges—who was eighty years old—failed to vote in favor of the transfer, another raised his hand for him. Laszlo immediately appealed against the transfer.

In a surprise move, the judgment was overturned, despite behind-the-scenes scheming by the Securitate. Laszlo was delighted. The case brought the attention of the whole Reformed Church in Transylvania to Laszlo's struggle. A thirty-one-year-old pastor of the Dej congregation could command 4,000 signatures in his support, despite pressure from the corrupt church leadership and the Securitate!

Laszlo's victory was short-lived. The bishop—supported all along by his faithful lay co-chairman, Gyula Tunyogi—ignored the ruling and church law and transferred Laszlo anyway. The place he chose was the isolated village of Sinpetru de Cimpie, to the east of Cluj. There Laszlo would be out of the way.

Laszlo had no objection to serving in a small and remote village. Indeed, one of his greatest loves was traditional Transylvanian village culture. He retained fond memories of the childhood days he had spent in Szentmarton. Under ideal circumstances, he would have been happy in such a small village, removed from the problems of the towns: a quiet life of hard work, dedicated to the people he loved.

But Laszlo refused to accept the bishop's decision to transfer him. The bishop had no right to transfer an assistant pastor who had been elected permanently to his post by the council of elders. The Reformed Church laid down the autonomy of the congregation. When it came to principle, Laszlo was unyielding. However, the Securitate meddled in this intra-church affair. The minutes of the 1983 meeting when Laszlo was elected had been sent to the relevant higher church bodies, but—apparently— were never received. Claiming that Laszlo had never been appointed permanently to the Dej congregation, the bishop suspended him.

A second delegation traveled to Cluj to see Bishop Nagy. The people were determined to keep Laszlo. Ten members of the first delegation were too afraid to go, after the Securitate's threats. But twelve more joined the other thirty. This time they caught the bishop unawares. "You have no right to remove Laszlo," they told him. Nagy was uneasy and tried to slip away from the group. But they surrounded him to prevent him from running away. Yet the visit had no effect. The Securitate was behind him.

Laszlo's last service in the Dej church was on Sunday, May 12, 1984. Pastor Laposi even started legal proceedings against Laszlo to force him to vacate his room in the church-owned house. Having lost his job, Laszlo also lost his home. He tried to resist the order and stay put but eventually had to leave. He returned to his parents in Cluj.

The Dej congregation continued to pay him the same amount he received when he was working there. In addition, faithful members of the community pressed all kinds of gifts on him. His family, too, lent their support. But Laszlo would take only what he had received before, in spite of their protestations.

That time was also difficult for some of Laszlo's colleagues. Janos Molnar, one of his closest friends from seminary days, was arrested that month, beaten and tortured. Molnar was just one of eight Reformed clergymen to be targeted by the authorities.

Another pastor, Janos Sipos from the village of Laran near Satu Mare, died under mysterious circumstances in autumn, 1984. He had just attended a deanery meeting in the town of Carei and had walked to the bus station to catch his regular bus home. It did not appear that day, so he had to hitchhike. He was soon picked up by a big truck, and that was the last he was seen alive. Two weeks later, his body was found at the bottom of a lake near Bucharest, on the other side of the country. He was opposed to the government's policy of assimilating the Hungarian minority but was not known as being an opposition activist.

His case was never properly investigated. The authorities said Sipos had committed suicide, but how his body came to be discovered 300 miles away was never explained. It looked like the work of the Securitate. His poor wife—who was unemployed—and their four young children were left penniless. Members of the Reformed Church collected money for the family, until they were stopped by Bishop Papp. They did manage to buy the family an apartment.

Back Home Again

Two years without work followed for Laszlo. While the Dej congregation continued their battle to take Laszlo back, he began the long and dispiriting path on his own. The Dej congregation was obliged to find a successor. But they did so only under duress. They had to invite applications for the post but showed no enthusiasm for the new applicants. When the day of the election came, the congregation gathered in the Gothic church for the vote. Unanimously, they declared their choice for Laszlo.

Afterward the chairman, looking discomfited, addressed the faithful. They should choose a better direction. Half the congregation immediately walked out. The other half cast their votes. The applicant who came in second was appointed as assistant pastor. He had gained just sixty-eight votes out of a total congregation of 4,000.

All did not go well for Laszlo's former boss, though. Jozsef Laposi, who was not only the pastor of Dej but also the local dean, had become unpopular with the congregation because he cooperated with the bishop in Laszlo's removal. Under popular pressure, he had to relinquish his post as pastor.

Laszlo was determined to continue his battle to be reinstated. The congregation had freely chosen him and that was where he would remain. But he did not begin this struggle out of hotheadedness. He knew he could do so only with the support—both moral and financial—of his people.

Besides, his battle was not just for his own ministry but also to uphold the rights of the individual against corrupt authority, whether of the church or of the state.

He was as firmly opposed to what he saw as clerical dictatorship as he was to state oppression. Bishop Nagy was breaking the laws of his own church, although his job was to uphold them.

During this time, Laszlo was living with his parents back in Cluj. He spent his time visiting his friends and studying. The apartment, in the shadow of the seminary and Cluj's famous Twin Towers church, was owned by the Reformed Church. Istvan cheekily wrote to the bishop's office asking for a reduction in the rent. He said that, if there were more family members living in the flat, the regulations prescribed that the rent should be reduced. Bishop Gyula Nagy wrote back to say that Laszlo was not a member of the family.

Having no congregation, Laszlo thought of further study abroad. So he signed up for the exams at the seminary. It was his dream to study at Princeton, but although he scored highest out of almost twenty in the qualifying exam, he was refused permission. The bishop and the Securitate did not allow him to go. Others went to study abroad in his place.

So he pursued his studies at home. He wrote articles, some of which were published in the *Reformed Review* or in East Germany. The themes he chose, all practical, show his main concerns—pastoral theology, liturgy and how to preach. Other articles by Laszlo remained unpublished and exist only in manuscript. The censor did not allow all of them to see the light of day. He also wrote an article on the history of the church during the Reformation. This reflective period was very different from his previous life in Brasov or Dej, where he had thrown himself into community work. Nor would he have time to study and write later, in Timisoara. This tranquil period of study was a quiet interlude.

No pastor in Cluj dared to invite Laszlo to preach. All of them knew him, and some would have liked to invite him, but they were afraid.

A Resolute Girl

The one bright spot for Laszlo during this time of troubles was his romance with a young native of Dej, Edith Joo. A resolute girl, a teacher by profession, she was increasingly drawn into his battle. When she was summoned to the Securitate and pressured to break off the engagement, they told her Laszlo was nothing more than a rogue. The next day they called at her father's house. They told him to pressure Edith to break off the relationship, warning that it would ruin her life.

The Securitate also revived rumors about Laszlo's private life. Anonymous letters were sent, wondering why this thirty-three-year-old pastor had still not married. They hinted darkly at "moral reasons" and claimed he had devastated a Brasov girl with a promise of marriage.

But Edith knew the man she had chosen. She would not be intimidated. She had first come to know Laszlo soon after he arrived in Dej, while she was still a student. But she was soon off to teacher training college in Baia Mare, a town in the north of Romania. After a time away, they were not so close, but when she returned Laszlo knew he was in love. After graduating in 1983, Edith had to begin a three-year teaching stint at a place chosen by the authorities. Hungarians were often sent to Romanian areas. Edith went to a town in Moldavia on the far side of the Carpathian mountains.

As they prepared for marriage, Laszlo's situation looked hopeless. There seemed no prospect of returning to work in Dej. The state and the church were conspiring against him, using every weapon at their disposal. The pressure on Edith was the hardest to bear. Laszlo remembered the fate of the prophet Jeremiah. With his country falling, he was imprisoned. Yet, demonstrating faith in the future, he bought a small parcel of land from his prison cell. This was, Laszlo believed, the guiding force of his fiancée. Superficially, it seemed she was making a bad marriage. It would bring nothing but trouble, as the Securitate kept reminding her. But she had faith and hope in the future.

The wedding day—December 15, 1985—was a moment of hope and light in a grim day-to-day existence. It was a manifestation of hope. The new pastor of Dej applied for special permission for Laszlo's father Istvan to conduct the service in the Dej church. Once again, Laszlo stood in the church at the front of the congregation—but this time as bridegroom.

Many guests were invited. The church was full. Laszlo and Edith made sure there were friends present from all the places they had known. People gathered from far and wide to share the day. The literary group from Dej was there, as well as the majority of Laszlo's former congregation. Everyone who came was aware of the risks involved: accepting the invitation meant identifying with Laszlo's cause. The wedding was in traditional Transylvanian style, with a lively celebration afterward.

After the marriage, Edith had to return to her teaching

post in far-off Moldavia. The authorities would not allow her to leave her job and move back to Laszlo. Her compulsory three-year work stint had to be completed. She left the following summer when the three years were up, but the school refused to let her go voluntarily. Without papers from the school, she would find it almost impossible to get another job.

Just as Laszlo was determined to resist Bishop Gyula Nagy's illegal action, so Istvan, too, fought his own battle. Istvan told the bishop he did not receive his permission to work from him but directly from God.

Laszlo had continued his campaign for reinstatement by starting a one-man demonstration outside Bishop Nagy's office. He persistently turned up day after day, but Nagy always refused to see him. As news of it spread, Laszlo's little public performance was a major source of embarrassment to Nagy. But still he would not offer Laszlo a job.

That December, U.S. Secretary of State George Shultz was in Bucharest, where he met the Romanian leaders. Little did Laszlo know about what these international statesmen were discussing. But Shultz had a list with him of human rights cases the American government was following. Could this have led to some movement in Laszlo's case?

An Unexpected Offer

In January, 1986, an unexpected visitor appeared at Istvan's door in Cluj—with an unexpected question. It was one of Bishop Laszlo Papp's assistants. Did he think Laszlo would accept a job in his church district? Papp obviously wanted to sound Istvan out before he offered a job directly to Laszlo.

The two bishops—both of them collaborators with the regime—had never gotten along. Of the two, Papp was more widely despised than his colleague. Bishop Gyula Nagy of Cluj did at times at least try to avoid carrying out the state's dirty work. He had removed Laszlo from his church in Dej but did not persecute the clergy with such apparent relish as Papp.

Laszlo Papp held services rarely, and almost never visited churches in his district. He was also an enthusiastic member of the Socialist Democracy and Unity Front in Bucharest, a pro-government body that was supposed to unite the country behind the Communist regime.

Papp's cooperation with the Securitate was active. It increased after four of his five children left the country— illegally. Three of them went to Hungary, the fourth to France. Papp was nervous about this sign of family disloyalty to the Communist regime and perhaps tried to compensate for it by working even more closely with the authorities.

So Laszlo and Istvan agreed to meet Papp to discuss the appointment. They took the train to Oradea and went to the bishop's office. Papp received them as honored guests. Laszlo and Istvan were wary at this sudden display of gentility. Papp talked about old times with Istvan and how they had studied together in seminary. He told them how he did not trust his fellow-bishop, Gyula Nagy. Behaving like a benevolent uncle, he offered Laszlo what he called a "new chance." He didn't tell Laszlo what he had in mind, only that it was a large university center. He wanted to see Laszlo's undoubted talents used for the good of the Church. "You're such a good pastor," he told him, "you should not go just to a small village."

But he issued a veiled warning. Laszlo should drop his old friends who had done so much damage to his career. If he did so, a brilliant future would unfold for him in the Church. Laszlo was bewildered by these confusing signals. He wanted to work again to serve his people. But how could he trust Bishop Papp? On the way home from Oradea, he stopped off near where Janos Molnar lived. In the dead of night he sneaked over to Janos's house.

What should he do? Should he accept a job? Janos warned him to be wary of Papp's tricks. But he had to take the chance—he would never be offered any other job. He should see what would happen. Laszlo mulled it over in his mind.

He was surprised when the bishop directly offered him the post of assistant pastor in Timisoara. The congregation was dead—everyone knew that. But to place a troublesome pastor in a place with such potential. . . . The bishop's famous cunning must have deserted him. Laszlo set some conditions but in the end had to take the job. He knew he would get no other offer.

The pastor of the Timisoara congregation was Leo Pauker. Laszlo believed Pauker was chosen to be his jailer.

SIX

A New Beginning

The strange manner of Laszlo's appointment to the Timisoara church gave him pause for thought. He soon realized the bishop had sent him there deliberately. Leo Pauker, said to be the most corrupt pastor in the whole church district, was a potential replacement for Papp himself. Papp was already nervous about his position with the authorities and wanted to neutralize his rival. What better way than to send a turbulent pastor who would bring him nothing but trouble? Papp could neutralize two troublemakers in one go. The sordid scheming sickened Laszlo.

Even more striking was the decay in the life of the congregation he saw when he arrived in July, 1986. From the way Pauker treated him and the miserable state of the parish, Laszlo had no doubt as to why this congregation had been chosen.

There were 10,000 Reformed Christians in Timisoara. On a good Sunday, fifty would attend Sunday services. Often it was much less. Pauker held no weekday services and sometimes even held no Sunday service. There was no religious instruction for children, no Bible study, no services to mark Holy Week. He had only five pupils for confirmation each year.

Leo Pauker had presided over this decline. With a checkered past, he enjoyed little respect in the community. He had begun training for the priesthood at the Catholic seminary in Timisoara, which was later closed by the Communists in 1947. However, before reaching ordination, he left to join the Reformed Church, where he later became a minister. His non-Reformed background made some members of the congregation wonder where he really stood. On top of this, his openly acknowledged allegiance to the Communist Party increased suspicion. In the 1950s, people say, he preached with a red star on his clerical gown. The state heaped official honors on him.

It was a depressing prospect for Laszlo as he moved in—without Edith. The Church leadership must have assumed there would be no opportunity here for Laszlo to resume his troublesome activities. At a stroke, the bishops seemed to have solved their problem with this turbulent pastor by dumping him in a dead parish where he would be isolated and unable to build up support.

At the end of the school year in June, Edith joyfully returned from Moldavia to Dej, back to her parents, hoping to join Laszlo in Timisoara right away. She was already expecting their first baby. But the authorities refused her the necessary permission to join her husband.

As Pauker directed Laszlo to the tiny room adjacent to the sanctuary, which was to be his new home, it was clear the role Pauker expected him to play. Although the Church owned a number of apartments, Pauker refused to give one to Laszlo. He was not allowed to hold services in the main church. He was given a small chapel on the edge of Timisoara to look after. This chapel had room for only thirty people.

Laszlo decided to bide his time. He was determined to revive this dead parish but knew it would take time. He listened to what he was told by the leadership but did not do what they wanted. Yet he remained polite and aloof. He wanted to build up the congregation first.

The authorities still did not allow Edith to join him there. She had to remain in Dej. In the time leading up to the birth of their first child, Laszlo was hardly able to visit her. There was the long distance and also the obstacles put in his way by the authorities. Visitors were surprised to notice that when he was out on the street he was always alert—watching for signs of being followed. He constantly looked over his shoulder. He had to be ready for anything.

After Mate was born, Edith finally received permission to join Laszlo. But he and his growing family still had only one room to live in, plus a toilet. They had no bathroom. Edith had nowhere to take their son Mate when he cried, and he would often disturb the Sunday services. Pauker's wife kept telling Edith: "You should stop your child's crying!" The whole congregation was angry at the way Pauker was treating their new pastor and his family. The people were especially incensed when Pauker moved his son into a vacant three-room apartment owned by the Church to prevent it from being given to Laszlo.

The young family remained in their cramped, unhealthy room, and Mate continued to cry. Pauker grew more and more angry at this until finally, during the Christmas, 1986, service, he had a stroke. He was immediately rushed to the hospital, where he died a few days later. Pauker's widow never forgave Laszlo. One Sunday after the service, she screamed at Laszlo for all to hear, "You're a murderer!"

Laszlo was left in sole charge of the congregation. Even Bishop Papp recognized this. He tried to co-opt him by showing great attention to him. Papp realized his colleague Bishop Nagy had achieved nothing by persecuting Laszlo. At this stage Papp was still trying to control him by giving him latitude. He thought Laszlo would be grateful to him.

Laszlo held his first service in the main church on January 1, 1987. Although he was in charge, the bishop prevented him from becoming full pastor. This meant that the bishop's office retained the power to remove him at will. The job of pastor was never filled. Although there was a shortage of Reformed pastors in Ceausescu's Romania, this was a common trick. Many pastors remained for years with only the status of assistants. It created uncertainty and kept pastors in their place.

Later, in 1987, Papp would offer to give Laszlo the full pastorship—if the congregation renounced its right to choose its own pastor. Laszlo refused, believing that the congregation should not sign away this time-honored right.

The Long Battle

A wide spiral staircase with peeling plaster led up from the church office and pastor's apartment to the church. The church's austere interior was dominated by a central pulpit at the front. When Laszlo ascended the steep stairs to it each Sunday, he towered above the congregation. Below the pulpit were the simple communion table and rows of wooden benches. Along one side of the church stood large tiled stoves.

Laszlo began his long battle to revive the congregation. Numbers gradually rose as word traveled that a new pastor had taken over. What was more, he was dynamic, uncorrupted and preached well. There was no immediate dramatic influx of people, but numbers for confirmation rose, as did the parish income. New cards were gradually added to the file of church members in the parish office. After twenty years of stagnation, the church was slowly coming to life.

Laszlo worked hard to build up his congregation. He inspired strong affection and devotion from his people. This was not just because of his sufferings: he was dedicated to a renewal of church life in his congregation. He risked the wrath of the state and of Bishop Papp to hold youth services, inspiring young people to take part in drama and worship. He believed, too, in direct and fearless preaching—many people who were not even church members came to his church to hear his sermons. It was not for nothing that his second-favored career was to be a teacher.

Laszlo's preaching was his life. He had a way of speaking directly to his congregation that made his words relevant to their everyday lives. It was as though he were talking to each member of the congregation. He preached for about thirty-five or forty minutes. People said that was always too short. His sermons were imbued with quotes from the Bible as well as from famous Hungarian authors. Thus his preaching meant something to both the simple and the intelligent. Listening to his preaching was like taking a shower, one member of the church declared.

His magnetic personality soon drew people into more active membership in the church. He was especially popular with the young people. More and more came to his religious instruction classes. But, as in Dej, Laszlo tried to involve the young people in the worship of the church. During Advent and Christmas, the children's choir sang and children recited poems. All this had been common in Reformed churches before the war, but the Communists had stamped it out.

Timisoara was a university town, and students from all over Romania studied there. Soon they started coming to his services. As Laszlo's fame and influence spread in the town, Bishop Papp must have regretted his decision to place him in Timisoara. A spontaneous ecumenical community grew up as students of other religions— Catholics, Protestants and Orthodox Romanians—began to regard the church as their own. Laszlo also developed links with other clergymen and communities in the city, especially the Baptists. He became good friends with Erno Neumann, the local rabbi.

It was only after Laszlo arrived that most people learned of his problems with the authorities in Dej. When he was appointed, few knew of his turbulent past. Laszlo worked hard for his flock, rarely putting in less than a twelve-hour day. He always had time for people and had a kind word for each. The people showed their affection for him and his family by showering them with gifts. Even in shortage-ridden Romania, they brought him chickens, vegetables and cakes.

The "Era of Light"

As the 1980s wore on, the shortages in Romania got worse. Ceausescu was meeting increasing criticism abroad for his human rights record and was set on a course of isolating Romania from the world. Like other Eastern European nations, he had borrowed money on easy terms from the West to build up Romanian industry. Now, in the harsher climate of the 1980s, other states were begging for delays in paying back the money and asking for further loans. Not Ceausescu. Full of pride for himself and his country, he was determined to start paying back the loans. In full. As Romanians starved in their unheated homes, precious food and industrial goods were shipped abroad in exchange for Western currency. The standard of living plummeted in what Ceausescu fondly called "the era of light."

Electricity shortages turned into long blackouts as power was switched from homes to factories. Street lighting was cut, until Romanians were wandering around in the gloom at night. Gasoline shortages—in a country that has its own oil supply—brought rationing of about four gallons per month. But the food and heating shortages hit people hardest.

Families would sit huddled in one room in winter, wearing blankets or coats to keep warm. In apartment buildings—most with a central heating system—the temperature rarely rose above 6 degrees centigrade (43 degrees Fahrenheit) in winter.

Rationing began in about 1975 and gradually spread to more and more foods. Adults were allowed half a loaf of bread per day, and each month, one pound of meat, a pint of cooking oil, ten eggs, two pounds of flour and two pounds of butter—when the shops had any of these. More often than not, even these supplies were not available. Coffee was last seen in Romanian shops in the early 1970s. The party leaders were, of course, exempt from such privations. They lived a life of luxury in sumptuous houses.

Finally, in 1989, Ceausescu announced with great fanfare that Romania had paid back all its foreign currency loans. As the people froze and starved, it was hardly something to be grateful for.

Ever since his rise to power in 1965, Nicolae Ceausescu had built up an extraordinary personality cult. As he consolidated his power and removed his rivals one by one, Romania became his personal kingdom. He and his wife Elena portrayed themselves almost as king and queen. Their photographs were everywhere, newspapers and television were required to give extensive coverage to their every action and Ceausescu's speeches became longer and longer. People gradually gave up reading the Communist press, since whatever information there had once been was now giving way to more and more fanciful eulogies to the president. Television, which only broad-

cast for about four hours a day because of the power shortages, became hardly worth watching.

Whenever Ceausescu traveled to a different town—
which he did with unnerving frequency—smiling and
cheering crowds were dragooned into attending. Teachers feared the consequences if their pupils failed to greet
the great leader with sufficient enthusiasm. Giant portraits of the dictator were issued to the public at parades.

Ceausescu's cult of personality grew more and more
oppressive until people almost believed there was something demonic in his power. Even in private, people were
reluctant to talk about Ceausescu directly—and not only
for fear of the Securitate. There was a strong dislike of
even uttering his name. His hold on the people was a
mixture of hatred, terror and almost demonic oppression.

No hint of opposition or criticism was allowed. The few
dissidents to speak out were imprisoned or exiled. Even
former leading Communists were often banished to ob-
scurity. As opposition activists in most Eastern European countries grew more bold, they continued to be
silenced with severity in Romania. Together with isola-
tionist Albania, Romania seemed immune to such stir-
rings of free speech.

With an ever-present secret police, ordinary Romanians did not dare complain openly. There was a widespread belief that a quarter of the population acted as
informers. People believed that telephones contained hid-
den Securitate microphones. Whether true or not—and
the extent of Securitate activity during the Ceausescu
era may never be known—few Romanians escaped without some unpleasant contact with the security organs.

Ceausescu was determined to keep the whole population on a tight leash.

In the 1980s, Ceausescu's plans became more fanciful as he gradually lost touch with reality. He had visions of creating a Romanian superrace. His wife decreed that all women should have at least four children to increase the population from its level of 23 million. The population was moved around in order to assimilate the various national minorities. And, most visible of all, plans were drawn up in both towns and villages to replace all old housing with new tower blocks. Starting in Bucharest, the capital, old districts were destroyed and new avenues were laid out with modern apartment houses.

Far from being idyllic, the apartments incorporated all the worst aspects of modern housing estates that, by this time, were a thing of the past in the West. The apartments broke up communities and housed people in anonymous blocks where people knew no one. They prevented people from keeping their own animals for food in their little gardens. They looked ugly. But what was worse was the miserable building standards. Many people were forced to move in even before construction was finished. And no one bothered to clean up the new districts, so that many still looked like building sites decades after being built.

Bucharest's nineteenth-century charm—the city was once known as the Paris of the Balkans—was largely destroyed in the wholesale rebuilding. Many of the homes bulldozed were old and somewhat primitive, but the vast expense involved did not result in better accommodation. Churches and historical monuments had to make way for the new boulevards.

In the center of the city, Ceausescu started building an enormous House of the Republic, which dwarfed everything around. While Bucharest sat in darkness, workers toiled night and day to build this graceless monstrosity. Ceausescu's delusions of grandeur required buildings of an imperial scale.

Many towns suffered needless rebuilding. Historic districts, which required no more than minimal modernization, were replaced with towering tenements. But it was the plan to remodel the countryside that finally brought protests into the open.

Ceausescu formulated a plan to bulldoze 7,000 of Romania's estimated 13,000 villages. Churches and religious monuments would be destroyed. Even more important, living congregations of the faithful would be dissolved as village folk were transferred to new "agro-industrial complexes." Workers would be employed in both industrial and agricultural work. The government claimed it would release more land for farming to ease the food shortages and provide better facilities for inhabitants.

Many people feared this plan. It would eventually destroy the separate identity of country people and merge them into the industrial working class. Old traditions, homes and cultures would be destroyed. Those who feared the plan the most were members of Romania's minorities, especially the Hungarians. They believed the plan was conceived with the aim of destroying Hungarian village life in Transylvania. The community of Szeklers, which was fiercely proud of its separate identity, feared annihilation.

But organized protest within Romania was non-existent. There was no way of expressing public opposition to a plan people detested. Laszlo felt impelled by his faith and his conscience to speak out. He loved the old Hungarian culture that would be destroyed in this plan. His almost sentimental attraction to village life made him feel the loss keenly. But it was more than that. He saw the plan as an attack on the whole population. Soulless living conditions would destroy people's lives. Laszlo believed that it was the role of the church to take a lead, even in such political matters. But he could not expect the church leadership to condemn the government's plans.

Stopping the Bulldozers

Laszlo was pleased with the development of the Timisoara congregation. But he felt that the situation in Romania was becoming critical. Yet what could one man do on his own?

One day in the spring of 1988, Laszlo called on his old friend from seminary days, Janos Molnar. Janos was now working as a pastor in Sebis, in the same Arad deanery. Janos had been constantly harassed for his outspokenness. As punishment, the bishops had moved him around from place to place, always sending him to the worst congregations. Soon after he graduated from the Cluj seminary, Janos was approached by the Securitate, who sought his cooperation as a spy. He refused. They then warned him that his wife Irma would never be allowed to work as a teacher. The Securitate would see to that. If he cooperated, though, he would receive a good congregation, and his wife would get a good job.

For fourteen years Janos was moved around, spending no more than two years in each place. He was sent mainly to Romanian villages with small Hungarian Reformed populations. He had small, aging congregations and few resources. Some of his congregations had not been financially self-sufficient for a very long time. But Janos worked hard and tirelessly, building up these small village congregations. He repaired the decrepit churches and inspired new confidence in the communities. But each time, he was removed.

After his arrest because of his involvement with *Counterpoints,* Janos was out of a job for a whole year—neither bishop would give him a congregation. Irma, too, was without work, and the couple had to survive on the occasional English lessons Irma was able to pick up. They had to move back to her parents' home in Tirgu Mures. After a while, the Securitate came to Irma and told her that she had no right to live in the city—even though her identity papers gave her place of residence as Tirgu Mures.

Finally Bishop Papp phoned Janos and said he could work again as a pastor only if he agreed to go to Sebis, a tiny village about seventy miles from Arad. If he refused to take the job, he would no longer be a pastor. Without a job he could be arrested as a "parasite." Having no job in Romania, even if prevented from working by the authorities, could result in a prison term of up to six months. Janos accepted and arrived in Sebis in 1984.

But harassment did not cease. The Securitate staged a car "accident" in which Janos and Irma could have been killed. It was a clear attempt to frighten them. They had had enough of Romania. Irma was afraid of going schizophrenic with the strain of life in Romania. She was beginning to have nightmares. They decided to apply to leave the country and go to Hungary. In the passport office, they were told it could take three or four years.

That spring day Janos and Laszlo talked for hours. Janos felt the same as Laszlo about the need to act. They reached an agreement on a plan of action. They would organize a concerted protest in all the deaneries of the Reformed Church, all of which met simultaneously each month. They would draft a protest against the village "systematization" program, which would be read at each deanery meeting in September. Janos believed that only an open, organized protest would have any effect.

This was no easy decision. Speaking out against systematization would risk Janos and Irma's last chance to leave Romania. But if they wrote a private letter to the bishop or President Ceausescu, the Securitate would be around the next day to arrest them just the same. Concerted action would give them some protection. Having reached the depths in Sebis, Janos felt he had nothing more to lose. He was prepared for radical action.

Laszlo was torn between the urge to speak out powerfully and the tactical need to do nothing so radical that it would jeopardize his new power base in Timisoara. Laszlo remembered well how powerless and ineffectual he was when unemployed for two years. Laszlo preferred a more subtle approach, arguing to Janos that it is sometimes better to give up your finger to survive. But gradually Janos's boldness inspired him to act.

The two conspirators agreed that Janos would read the protest at the Arad deanery pastors' meeting and take full responsibility for it. Laszlo promised to speak publicly in support of the protest, and if Janos were transferred or otherwise punished, he would immediately

organize a "trade union" of pastors and collect money to
support him and his wife.

Janos and Laszlo shook hands and set out to imple-
ment their scheme. Janos wrote four points attacking the
government's village demolition plan. Laszlo agreed with
Janos's words but added two further points of his own.
Since Janos did not have a typewriter—following the
1983 *Counterpoints* crackdown he had had to sell his and
had been banned from owning one—Laszlo took the document back to his office in Timisoara to type. Laszlo and
Janos knew the protest had to be carefully worded. It had
to be addressed solely to the Church leaders so that the
state would have no just cause for interference.

Through the summer, Janos and Laszlo mobilized support among the pastors. As Janos and Laszlo discussed
those pastors who might be expected to read the protest
at their deanery meetings, they could think of only six
out of about 250 in the Oradea church district. They had
a busy—but depressing—time traveling around from pastor to pastor. Janos took the Oradea church district, while
Laszlo went the rounds of the Cluj district, where he was
still well-known. They discovered many times that what
many pastors thought privately and what they would
dare to say in public were two different things. Even
more distressing were the pastors who covered up their
fearfulness with theological justification.

Nevertheless, by the end of the summer Janos and
Laszlo thought they had found a spokesman in nearly
every deanery.

Laszlo and Janos were acutely aware that the success
of the protest depended as much on publicity abroad as on
support in Romania. Janos gave a copy to an old and

trusted Dutch friend who visited Romania that summer. Laszlo left a copy with friends from Budapest. Their contacts would receive a coded telegram from them after the meeting to signal that the text had been read in the Arad deanery and that the mass media should be alerted. They had learned from their experience with *Counterpoints* that there would be sacrifices. But only international publicity would give them some degree of protection. Janos and Laszlo had to discuss their plans while walking around the streets. They feared there were microphones even in the yard.

The deanery meetings were fixed for September 6. The evening before, Laszlo and Janos met. Their plans—worked out over so many months—were ready for launch. Janos was already nervous. He still had not told Irma of the scheme, fearing the effect it would have on her. He didn't quite know how to bring up the subject. "Maybe I won't come home tomorrow," he finally told her. Irma read the memorandum for the first time. She was aghast.

SEVEN

On the Offensive

On September 6, 1988, Dean Jozsef Kovacs convoked the Arad deanery. He opened with prayer. Then minutes of the previous meeting were read. On and on the meeting went. Janos could not concentrate on the routine business at hand. His mind kept coming back to the statement he had in his pocket that, within a few minutes, he would be standing up to read. The meeting droned on, the accounts were read and discussed, various administrative measures were agreed upon and due consideration was being given to a number of possible future options for the Church. Janos could not concentrate. He hardly heard what people were saying.

At long last the meeting dragged to an end. Dean Kovacs was about to bring the proceedings to a close. Janos stood up. His stomach contracted. His shirtsleeves were wet with sweat. The faces of his colleagues turned toward him. He found it hard to breathe. In a quiet voice he asked the dean if he could say a few words. Trying desperately to stop his voice from trembling, he told the dean he had written a paper on a subject that was of concern to all the pastors and the future of the Church. The statement was addressed to the synods of the Oradea and Cluj districts. The dean said he could proceed.

Janos looked down at his paper and started to read. His legs were shaking. But in a steady voice he read through the six points, not knowing if he would be able to get through to the end.

Janos called on the national leadership of the Reformed Church to invite non-Reformed religious leaders in Romania to plan a coordinated dialogue with government officials responsible for the systematization plan. "The destruction of villages means the destruction of the past," Janos told the assembled pastors. "Any people would become rootless if its past were wiped off the face of the earth."

The dean's jaw dropped as he heard the statement. He sat rooted to his chair, his eyes bulging like a frog's. He was white. The other pastors were quiet, hardly believing their ears. As Janos stumbled to the end and sat down, everyone was silent for a moment.

Already primed on the subject, Laszlo rose to speak in favor. Laszlo proposed that at Sunday services each Reformed congregation should pray by name for villages earmarked for destruction. He said that in Timisoara he and the congregation had for a long time been praying to stop the demolitions. One pastor jumped up and said there should immediately be a vote on who was for and who against. "It is the main problem facing us now. We must take a stand." He then went forward to sign the memorandum. Other pastors immediately followed.

The pastors voted overwhelmingly for the motion. The vote was fifteen in favor, while four abstained. There were no votes against. Seven pastors were absent from the meeting. Janos and Laszlo were surprised at the courageous response of those present. They had been expecting only some hesitant, muted support from three or four others. But fifteen had signed. And the four who didn't hadn't actually spoken against the motion. Even the dean hadn't spoken against it, although he had not dared to sign.

As Janos stood up to speak, he believed that in ten other deaneries his colleagues would be doing the same. But he was to be disappointed. Other deaneries failed to follow suit. At the Cluj deanery meeting, Pastor Endre Kozma started reading a statement protesting against the plans, but the dean immediately stepped in to stop him. The other pastors who said they would speak out stayed silent. Fear had overcome their courage.

Immediately after the meeting, an informer among the pastors reported to the Securitate. Janos had deliberately not given out copies of the memorandum. But he knew the Securitate would hear very soon. The Department of Religious Affairs phoned Bishop Papp from Bucharest and told him to bring in Janos and Laszlo for questioning at the bishop's office. A Securitate officer from Bucharest was dispatched at once to Oradea to find out what had happened.

The Securitate immediately started visiting those who had signed the memorandum. All their questions were about Janos. Did Janos organize the action? Was it a conspiracy? Was he the ringleader? How had he organized it? They asked all of them when they had first heard about the attack on the systematization plans. The pastors replied truthfully—the first they had heard was when Janos got up to read his statement in the meeting.

The hapless dean, Jozsef Kovacs, was hauled in by the Securitate in Arad for failing to control the meeting. Those in authority in the churches were made to take responsibility for disobedience lower down. Kovacs told them he had not known in advance what Janos would read. He mumbled that he had been very tired and wasn't able to think properly. He must have had some kind of mental block. The secret police did not believe that Kovacs did not know in advance. They asked the clerk in his office to listen in on the dean's phone calls and report his conversations if there was any evidence that he had prior knowledge of the protest.

The Man With Red Socks

The two offenders were summoned to Oradea on Friday morning, just three days after the meeting. The bishop's offices were turned into an interrogation center. The calm, stately rooms were threatening and hostile. The civilized surroundings were at odds with the unseemly business going on. Janos and Laszlo were locked in separate rooms. Each had a guard. The guard followed them, even into the bathroom. The two were interrogated separately but simultaneously.

The Securitate tried to make Laszlo declare that his friend and colleague was a tool of Western spies. The agent claimed Janos had not written the text himself. He knew Laszlo had typed it. Other people in the West had written it. Or maybe Laszlo's father, Istvan. The man worked hard to try to convince Laszlo. "Why do you think Janos is not capable of writing such a memorandum?" Laszlo asked them. "He's educated, articulate, and he's a poet. And he's a good pastor. He could have written it himself."

The bishop butted in: "I've warned you not to associate with Janos Molnar."

"Why not?" Laszlo asked. "What do you have against him? Is he an alcoholic? Is he immoral?"

Bishop Papp was furious, at a loss for words. Finally he spluttered, "He doesn't dress like a dignified pastor. He wears red socks."

The bishop and the Securitate had no copy of the protest, even three days after the meeting. Janos had been told on the phone to bring the text with him so that they could examine it. The Securitate officer spoke no Hungarian, so Janos—sitting next to the bishop—had to translate it into Romanian. As they studied the text, the bishop and the Securitate officer came to the conclusion that there was nothing in it against the state. Janos's careful wording had seen to that. Even so, he was surprised at the mildness of the response.

Janos was even more surprised at the change that had come over Papp. He had always seemed arrogant. Now he looked embarrassed and even frightened. He treated Janos almost with respect. "What do you hope to solve by this attitude?" he asked him. "God doesn't need your help."

Janos replied, "All through history God has worked through human beings."

Papp had no answer. But he showed little concern for the possible loss of church buildings caused by the village destruction program. "Believers can pray in the open air, or in a cellar. To practice your faith you don't need a church." This was Bishop Papp's attitude.

At the end of the interrogation, Janos was told the memorandum would be passed on to the "proper organs" —the secret police—for a translation. They would make a decision on further action.

Laszlo and Janos had been right. The Securitate did not know how to tackle this coordinated revolt. Had Janos read the memorandum on his own, they could have arrested him, deported him or even killed him. But even the Securitate did not know how to cope with a protest signed by so many "rebels" in the Arad deanery.

Janos's coordinated and courageous stand had at last put the issue of systematization on the agenda within an official body in Romania. The church was the only institution that could still register its opposition to unjust government policy, however feebly. And he had shown that the government was reluctant to move against a coordinated opposition. Laszlo noted the lessons.

But if they thought their condemnation of the systematization plans would stir the Church into action, they were disappointed. Their initiative, while admired secretly, was an isolated instance of protest. Theirs was the only one of thirteen deaneries to speak up. Pastors were afraid to lose their congregations.

The action also brought a tightening of state control at the meetings. Before, government officials attended only every third meeting. Now they attended every one. The inspector would lurk around the whole time, not even leaving the room during breaks. He was the first to arrive and did not leave until all the pastors had gone. He was afraid of missing anything.

Bishop Papp went on a tour of the deaneries and delivered a speech strongly attacking Janos and the memorandum. He was determined to prevent such revolts from spreading. By blackening Janos's name, Papp turned him into a hero. In some deaneries, such as Satu Mare in the far north of the country, they had hardly heard of the protest. Papp surprised them all with the news and, in the process, spread Janos's fame.

Janos was encouraged by the support of his flock. People all knew about his action. They were afraid that if they heard about it from Radio Free Europe the Securitate would come and kill him. Members of the congregation told Irma that, if Janos was arrested, she should not worry about how to survive. They would help. They were already bringing food and other gifts. And it was not only the Hungarians from the congregation. Romanians from the Orthodox Church also showed their support.

Janos paid dearly for his boldness. A few weeks after the meeting, he received a letter from the bishop. He was being issued a reprimand for his behavior. He was also banned from attending deanery meetings. But the state authorities were harsher. They were already wary of him—they had been keeping a close eye on him ever since his involvement in *Counterpoints* was discovered.

About the same time, Janos was summoned by the passport office. He was told there was no reason now that he could not leave. In fact, he and Irma should leave as soon as possible. The government had decided to get rid of Janos, so the Molnars received their passports in record time. Just before they left, they were warned not to forget that they had eaten Romanian bread for so long. Janos told them it was so bad it would take them a long time to forget it, even if they wanted to.

Meanwhile Laszlo's father, Istvan, was waging his own individual struggle against the corruption of the Reformed Church leadership. His campaign for the Church to adhere to its own constitution—begun by his 1979 letter to the Church's synod—was getting more urgent. The growing totalitarianism of the Ceausescu regime was reducing the democratic power of each congregation. The bishops were replacing this, at the urging of the state, with central authority. This went against all presbyterian principles.

In August, 1988, Istvan issued a statement, renewing his earlier attacks on the dictatorial running of the Church by the leaders. He accused them of "brutal arbitrary acts" that bypassed the proper constitutional running of the Church. He described the bishops as "marionettes"—a thinly veiled reference to the manipulation of Church officials by the Romanian state.

Istvan attacked the rigged elections, the uncanonical appointment of pastors, misinformation published by the Church bureaucracy, restrictions on the preaching of the Gospel, the uncanonical running of the seminary, the cult of personality around the two bishops and the illegal dismissal of active pastors.

The wholesale attack on the whole running of the Church by one of the Church's most knowledgeable members was based on Istvan's belief that this was what had caused its decline. He believed the Church could not be revived without a return to its presbyterian constitution. He called for a free General Synod to be convened at once. Yet, while he believed these administrative measures were necessary to renew the Church, Istvan did not put his sole hope in them. He demanded repentance on the part of the Church and an acceptance of the leading of the Holy Spirit.

Istvan Tokes received no reply from the Church leadership, but the declaration no doubt increased the anger of the bishops against him.

Truth and Theater in Timisoara

Several hundred people now took part regularly in the life of the Timisoara congregation. The members of the church were developing a great personal loyalty to their dedicated pastor. Through his preaching, Laszlo taught the people to resist evil authority, wherever it might manifest itself. Only truth would overcome. He gave his congregation courage in their own homes, their factories and schools.

Laszlo continued the cultural activities he had begun in Dej. On Reformation Day, October 31, 1988, he organized a literary evening in the church. The Thalia Theater, an amateur group made up of students at Timisoara University, were to take part. Before the event could take place, it was unofficially banned by the authorities—Laszlo was simply told that it should not take place. What concerned the authorities most was the involvement of young people. Laszlo was warned that students should not take part. "Who can, then?" he asked them. "No one," they replied. The students, too, were warned. But the event went ahead.

Laszlo and the Thalia group went ahead with a second such evening in December, in spite of a further unofficial ban. The students read religious and secular poetry in Hungarian. This time the authorities stepped in. The theater group was immediately dissolved. The blame was put on Laszlo. The Securitate hauled him in for questioning. Bishop Papp—always eager to do the state's bidding—condemned Laszlo.

In fact, the following month Papp tried to remove Laszlo from the parish. The Securitate obviously wanted him out of the way. The Romanian government had been reluctant to punish Laszlo publicly at the time for his part in the village destruction memorandum. At that moment, its human rights record was under close scrutiny by the West at the Vienna conference of the co-signatories of the Helsinki accord. But the close of this conference meant the end of the Ceausescu regime's good behavior. Now they were ready to move. Just as in Dej, the bishop was required to do the state's work.

But with the support of the church, Laszlo hung on. For two months the bishop tried all kinds of illegal methods of removing him. With a congregation of 500, Laszlo knew he was in a strong position.

Early in March, Laszlo got wind of unsettling news. Definite plans for his removal from the congregation in Timisoara had been leaked indiscreetly from the office of Bishop Papp.

Laszlo soon received a disturbing phone call. He was ordered to appear at the bishop's office March 9. There he was met by one of Bishop Papp's right-hand men, the Synodical Administrator Gyula Eszenyi. Eszenyi hurled humiliating abuse at Laszlo. He accused him of neglecting his congregation, holding forbidden church services, disrespecting his superiors and refusing to maintain the required relations with the state inspectors for religious affairs. The administrator used a Romanian folk saying to warn Laszlo: "The small lamb sucks from two ewes." The message was clear to Laszlo. He must suck for grace and favors from both the bishop and the state authorities if he wished to live unharassed. Eszenyi then confirmed that he was to be removed from Timisoara.

The storm against Laszlo was brewing again. While traveling to Tirgu Mures to visit his brother Andras, Laszlo was hauled off the train and detained on the pretext of suspected theft. A search of his possessions produced a few foreign periodicals and a copy of a letter he had sent to the World Alliance of Reformed Churches protesting against the village destruction policy. So this was what Eszenyi was talking about. Laszlo would have to please both the state and the church leadership or face dire consequences. He was not allowed to see his brother and was immediately sent back to Timisoara.

Concern in Canada

Stephen Tokes was an anxious man. He fully expected reprisals against his younger brother Laszlo after the reading of the memorandum against village destruction in Arad in September, 1988. The eldest of Istvan and Erzsebet's sons, Stephen fled Romania in 1968. After spending a year in Austria, he settled down in Canada. Stephen and his family prospered in Montreal, and he faithfully provided material support to his parents back in Transylvania. But now Laszlo was in deep trouble. Many citizens of the Socialist Republic of Romania faced an untimely death or imprisonment for acts far less grave than Laszlo's. Something had to be done, and quickly!

Having lived in the West for so many years, Stephen was aware of the power of the media and public opinion. He turned for help to a friend, the former Transport Minister of Quebec, Michel Clair. Michel, a French Canadian, had developed an interest in the nationality problems of Transylvania, which had some parallels with those of his native Quebec. Michel was prepared to undertake a risky and expensive journey to interview Laszlo on film. He took with him an experienced professional cameraman, Rejean Roy.

Through his trusted contacts in Hungary and Romania, Stephen made arrangements for the two journalists to travel clandestinely to Timisoara in March, 1989. It was a harrowing journey for the Canadians. They traveled separately as simple tourists. Rejean flew to Bucharest and went by train to Timisoara. Michel drove across the Hungarian frontier from Budapest. Their stomachs were in knots as they experienced the customarily long passport and customs checks upon entering Romania. But they reached Timisoara on Saturday night, March 18, without incident.

On Sunday morning they joined the crowd of faithful on their way to hear Laszlo preach at the Reformed Church. Inside the church, they discreetly approached Laszlo and whispered an identifying code word as they had been instructed by Stephen. Laszlo was relieved to discover that the visitors were genuine. In the past, the Securitate had tried to trick Laszlo into making incriminating statements by posing as sympathetic Western journalists or human rights activists. Laszlo told them to return with their cameras the following day.

On Monday morning, as the television crew lugged

their equipment up the winding staircase to the balcony of the Timisoara church, Laszlo knew what he was going to say. In a powerful tour de force, where careful words did not obscure his passion, he issued a stirring indictment of Ceausescu's village destruction policy and the silent acquiescence of his Church leaders.

EIGHT

Breaking the Wall of Silence

You see, gentlemen, I brought you here to the church for we dare not speak in our homes. According to a friend of mine, even my bathroom is bugged. I don't know if this is true, but in any case I am afraid to speak except outside, or in corridors. I do not dare to speak my mind even in church for, as far as I know, the church is monitored. I think that this morning, when no services are held, there is perhaps no danger.

You may wonder why I take the risk of talking to you. It is somewhat absurd, no doubt, for it is not only a sense of responsibility that makes me speak. I also have an irresistible urge to speak out at last, to say finally what I have so often wanted to say. I do not speak for myself, but instead of and on behalf of others. Why should we participate forever in this wall of silence? This wall is much more massive and impenetrable than

141

the Berlin Wall, and I feel somebody has to start to demolish it.

The other thing that induced me to take this step is not really new. As a matter of fact, I have carried on this activity for six years now, in public and in secret, conspicuously and unnoticed. As a minister, as a spiritual leader, I feel responsible to the people. This responsibility is even heavier, since most of my fellow ministers are silent.

I am a minister of the Reformed Church in Romania. The clergy, and in particular the bishops of this Church, identify completely with the policy which has, among other things, produced the mind-boggling plan to destroy the villages. Just imagine, gentlemen, when we submitted that letter in September, that petition to the bishops asking them to take up the cause of the villages, we were, all of us who had addressed the issue, summoned to the bishop's office, where a government inspector was present, too. The bishop, Laszlo Papp, eloquently argued for the scheme of countryside development—he even said it would be to our great advantage if some congregations disappeared with the resettled population. It is of no importance if the churches are pulled down, he said, for it is not the stones that matter but the services held inside them. To the dean he said, word for word: "Reverend, even if they pulled down the Reformed Church in Arad, people could still pray in meeting houses in the suburbs. Thus, even that would not be a loss we should bother about."

When I preach, I always try to find a connection between the present and the Scriptures, in particular in the extremely difficult situation we live in. I chose a passage for Palm Sunday from the Letter to the Philippians that could be applied to the present conditions if you read between the lines. When I spoke of the entrance of Christ into Jerusalem, I pointed out in my sermon, by way of contrast, that the world expects very different things from kings. Both the Bible and history furnish many examples of power turning the heads of kings and rulers. I mentioned the case of Nebuchadnezzar from the Old Testament, and—from modern history—Napoleon and Hitler, who had climbed up from below. In such cases power is even more dangerous and dizzying than it would be otherwise.

At the ministers' meeting in early September, I proposed that every minister of every congregation should pray for our villages and congregations, having in mind the village destruction plan. My colleague, Janos Molnar, who has now unfortunately crossed the border into Hungary, even made a written proposal that the Church administration should not look with folded arms while villages are destroyed, while the so-called "systematization" plan is carried out, but that it should contact the other churches, the Catholic Church, the Orthodox Church and others, in order to coordinate their views, to make it clear what the village destruction plan means for the churches, to find out how many congregations are affected and what the future holds for them.

On this matter, right now, there is perfect silence. It appears as if we are not at all concerned about what happens to hundreds of congregations, what happens to our churches (many of them centuries old), what happens to our cemeteries, where our people will be taken to from these settlements, and what the future holds for the Church and its members.

We summarized in a few points what the bishops— those of Cluj and Oradea—and other Church representatives should keep in mind in the course of negotiations with the state. These points were, roughly: the Church should suffer no losses as a consequence of the urbanization plan; they should follow the principle of keeping losses to the minimum, and when losses are unavoidable (e.g., when a village is to vanish, or the congregation resettled), there should be some form of compensation.

This is to say that the Church cannot just sit and accept what is happening. First of all, it should obtain information on what is being prepared, for the whole matter is wrapped in mystery, and only general slogans are being uttered. My fellow ministers and their congregations are personally affected, yet they are afraid to speak out. I feel that it is our duty to say all this, since everybody, in particular the Church hierarchy, is silent.

We decided therefore to bring up the proposal at a meeting where there were more people together, to build up our courage through joint action. We organized this action in the whole of the Reformed Church in Romania, in every deanery, all thirteen of them. There was in each place someone who took it upon himself to bring up this issue in the meeting of their deanery in early September.

It is sadly typical that there was only one deanery out of the thirteen where people had the courage to speak up. This shows clearly how fear affects even the ministers, though their very existence is at stake. After all, it is they who will lose their congregations, and they who will have to leave the place where they live.

The destruction of villages, or "countryside planning," does not take place in the "romantic" way that outsiders imagine, namely, that ten bulldozers show up and raze the village from one end to the other. It is more complex. Conditions must be created for the villages to vanish, accommodation must be assured for the inhabitants of the villages sentenced to death. All the more so as the wave of international protests has probably made them alter the original plans.

We cannot exactly tell what they were planning to do originally, for before the plan could truly get under way, the world raised a chorus of protest. It is impossible to tell how the destruction was to start and how the plans were changed afterward.

It appears now, and most probably this is true, that the scheme has not been abandoned. This is not a regime that would give up such a plan because of international protest. No, they have not given it up, only the methods have been changed. They try to conceal their plans by following the policy of wait and see, of tactical maneuvering, and of deceit. For example, some months ago they started to merge villages, which is hard to criticize. Normally, two, three or four villages constitute a municipality. Now they keep on merging them into larger units. Still more villages are attached to a municipality, thus making them lose their importance. These are generally the villages condemned to liquidation. They send out party officials and state bureaucrats to various villages, just like in the past, when they wanted to push collectivization of farms. They convene a meeting of the inhabitants or the party, where they present the question in such a way that the inhabitants themselves ask for the elimination of their village, for the possibilities of earning a living no longer exist.

I know of villages where people were made to sign a request to be resettled in apartment blocks to be built in the future.

Thus, instead of following a spectacular policy of village destruction, they apply the policy of atrophy, difficult to prove. For instance, the doctor of a village is removed, or a school with a small number of pupils is closed. This compels the children to go to school in another, larger settlement. Patients are forced to go to see the doctor in the neighboring village. Often they cut the electricity, or they reduce the supplies in shops. Thus the situation of the inhabitants becomes more and more hopeless, and they feel forced to leave the village. This is an infernal scheme indeed.

Actually, as far as the destruction of villages is concerned, it is much disputed even in this country whether it is happening or not. This is a pseudoproblem, many people say, for this massive plan cannot be carried out due to financial reasons. I would say, however, that the plan is quite realistic, for the destruction did not start now, nor at any time when the policy was declared. I think they made a great mistake in declaring it at all. In reality, it started years ago. For example in Cluj, in the Holstadt, a large part of the agricultural population— equal to the inhabitants of five or six villages—were removed from their homes and moved into apartment blocks, losing their gardens, houses, and rented land, which had assured their living.

Paradoxically, village destruction started in the cities long ago. Municipal districts the size of several dozen villages were destroyed over the past years and decades. Thus the trend is clear. The question is how far they can put their plan into practice, to what extent it can be implemented considering the state of the economy, and how much it will be influenced by international protest. And, let me add, how far God allows them to go, for by now we can place our trust only in God. The hymn by Martin Luther, "A mighty fortress is our God," has a special meaning in this connection. I could paraphrase it, adapting it to our present situation, as "A mighty fortress is our Church," for only our Church has been left to us.

I do not consider the role of ministers of outstanding importance, although our people have no other representatives at present whose intervention could carry similar weight. There is no denying that ministers can, or rather could, do a lot. Their voice is not only the voice of God but also the voice of the people, which is why I feel it was our professional duty to do what we did concerning this matter last September.

I would like to add that village planning, or as they officially call it, countryside planning, has a different meaning for the different nationalities. Romanians, even when protesting against it, stress different things than do we Hungarians. Of course, the Romanians are right to say that it is the concentrated masses of peasantry, not yet disintegrated, that stand in the way of this policy. The rural masses. Now it is their turn to be shaken up, dissolved, broken up and dispersed. This is also true. For the peasantry is essentially the only social class that has some material and moral base enabling it to oppose government policy.

What is important for us Hungarians at this time of extreme danger is that as a matter of fact, this is the last, or the next to last, phase of a process. Namely, during the past decades our institutions have been gradually and systematically wiped out, one after another. Our culture and our school system have been destroyed. An offensive has been conducted against all possible means of maintaining our ethnic identity, and I feel that it is now the churches' turn. They are now launching a frontal attack against the Reformed Church. And this applies to the Catholic Church as well as the Reformed, for practically the whole Hungarian population in Romania belongs to one of them.

As I say, we now see the last stage of this many-decades-old process, with an attack against the villages. There is a demographic aspect to this, too, for during the last decades they managed to Romanianize, partially or completely, Transylvanian towns with a Hungarian or German majority. Exact figures are not known, but 3 to 5 million Romanians have been settled here from beyond the mountains. Always from beyond the mountains. Israel is condemned for settling Jews among Arabs? That action is not less worthy of attention than what has happened here. In all our cities and towns whose population used to be 60 to 70 or 100 percent Hungarian, they pour in Romanian masses so as to upset the demographic equilibrium among the nationalities. Villages were the only places where they were helpless, for a Romanian from Moldavia or Wallachia would not come to settle in a Transylvanian village. That is why, in my view (which is not only mine), it is the villages that have now become their target. Now they want to dissolve and disintegrate these

Hungarian communities living in a massive, united ethnic block. The resettlement of villages, the mixing up of the population, is an excellent way to accomplish this, which is why I think this is the most important aspect of the question.

The destruction of villages actually has a subjective aspect, too, one that affects human rights. Something that cannot be measured, cannot be sensationalized around the world—and this is what is taking place in people's souls, affected as they are by disasters, family tragedies and spiritual defeat. One could only compare the situation to the 1950s, when—as we all know—people went through a period of hardship and were half-crippled spiritually. And now when they have started to raise their heads and to recover, when they can start to work and make up for their losses, another enormous action, such as collectivization at that time, is launched against them.

People have no choice, no way to protect themselves against this irresistible assault on them. What can people do? They can hang themselves—that is how some desperate people respond to this situation. Or they leave their native land. This stream of emigration, this helter-skelter flight eloquently shows what is going on here. There is much discussion as to whether we should or should not leave, whether we should stick it out, whether it makes any sense to stay. I often say that it is now beyond the level of verbal expression. Our situation can be compared to that of animals with a presentiment of danger, a volcanic eruption or an earthquake, when they just flee heedlessly. Nothing can help, neither arguments

nor sermons, for people just act as their momentary social and historical situation pushes them.

We find out everything that happens. Thus we know of
the protest letter by six Romanian former party leaders
addressed to Ceausescu. We learn of events from Hungarian radio and TV, whose programs are received not
only by the Hungarians living near the border but also
by Romanians and Serbians. We learn of those events,
and a strange situation emerges. A significant part of the
population reacts very emotionally to what they hear. In
their private life they find information, they discuss everything they hear or learn about. Yet they remain completely passive. Apart from the occasional comment
comparable to a guerrilla action, everybody expects the
solution to the problems—if they expect it at all—from
somebody else, or they expect problems to resolve themselves by natural evolution. There are also those who—I
must admit—are not at all aware of what is going on in
this context. This is related to their thinking and cultural level. Finally, there are those who do not react at
all to what is happening and who—if they know
anything—are taken in by daily platitudes and propaganda. Our attitude toward human rights is also very
particular. Because of our situation, we do not tackle the
issue of human rights according to the pure sense of the
word as used in the West, but rather according to our
particular social conditions. Here, human rights are
pushed into the background by collective rights, the
rights of the community. This is because in a totalitarian
regime people do not have the opportunity to protest
against individual human rights violations.

In a totalitarian system it seems to be a luxury to think

in terms of what I, as an individual, am or am not permitted to do. We have not yet reached the Western level of social development that would enable us to claim human rights as it is done in the Western, more highly developed world. Instead, we miss human rights in our collective existence. The question is not whether I, Laszlo Tokes, can or cannot do something, it is not that I, Laszlo Tokes, am deprived of freedom of speech, freedom of opinion, the right to free correspondence, the right to free association, or the right to instruction in my mother tongue, but I, a member of the Hungarian community.

Of course, I assume that this question comes up in a somewhat different way for Romanians, for the injustices they have to suffer are not rooted in national discrimination, thus human rights and collective rights are not so much interwoven as in our case. The rights stipulated by the basic document of the U.N. and by the Helsinki declaration are most brutally violated every day. If we do not speak more about them, it is because these people are as yet not aware of the human rights they are entitled to. Until they know what their rights are, we cannot speak to them of human rights. And we have not yet reached the level where at least we would know what our human rights are. I speak of the majority. Of course, there is a class of people, particularly in Transylvania, who are already aware of the human rights that they are deprived of.

NINE

Defiance

Laszlo crept back down to his office. Michel and Rejean tried to look like innocent tourists as they stepped onto the street. Now they had to perform a critical task: pass the videocassettes unobserved to two of Stephen's Hungarian contacts. The delivery went smoothly and the two Hungarians went their separate ways, one to Budapest by car, the other by train. Michel and Rejean breathed a sigh of relief once free of the potentially dangerous cassettes. With minds at rest, they set out for Cluj to interview Istvan. But the Securitate had been tipped off and intervened between the Canadians and Istvan's door. Here Michel and Rejean's mission came to an unceremonious end. They were obliged to leave Romania immediately. But by now the couriers and their precious cargo of videocassettes were safely in Budapest.

Back in Montreal, Stephen, Michel, and Rejean worked

furiously to translate and edit the tapes. They wanted the material to be of high quality and suitable for network TV. Their hard labor seemed to pay off. They had done a professional job. Now the world would see Laszlo on their TV screens. From now on, they thought, he would be protected by the mighty force of Western public opinion.

But they were mistaken. Their efforts to sell the video to a Canadian or American TV station were fruitless. No one was interested in this young, unknown Hungarian pastor. Nor was the media particularly alarmed by what was happening in faraway Romania. After all, the bloodthirsty dictator Ceausescu had won the respect of Western statesmen for his willingness to defy the Soviet Union, in particular his refusal to participate in the Warsaw Pact's invasion of Czechoslovakia in 1968. Perhaps this Communist maverick, the statesmen figured, could be manipulated to produce a breach in the apparently solid Soviet bloc.

President Nixon had invited him to Washington in 1973 amid much fanfare and publicity. Preferential trade arrangements were made with Romania. Queen Elizabeth bestowed the coveted Order of the Garter on the tyrant in a solemn ceremony at Buckingham Palace. And he was applauded for his religious policies: the Anglican Bishop of Southwark, the Right Reverend Mervin Stockwood, praised Ceausescu's "exceedingly generous" treatment of the Church. "We in Britain might well be envious," he declared. Evangelist Billy Graham's highly publicized 1985 Romanian crusade was a great public-relations success from the point of view of the Ceausescu regime. Graham thought it inappropriate to speak out against persecution.

Not surprisingly, week after week went by without a positive response from the media. Stephen got the same old story: "Thank you, but no thank you."

Waiting for the Bombshell

Laszlo knew he had taken a brave risk. His calm and carefully thought-out message would soon be broadcast all over the world. No one in Romania had managed to speak out so plainly and at such length to the outside world against any of Ceausescu's policies, let alone his cherished systematization scheme. Laszlo was eager to tell the world, whatever the risk might be to himself. He had to speak up in the name of his community as well as in the name of all citizens of Romania.

But Laszlo's eagerness turned to frustration as his bombshell languished unbroadcast in the West. No one would hear his *cri de coeur*. He had to continue his campaign without the expected help from the outside world. And the campaign to remove him was gathering steam.

Laszlo received an unwelcome birthday present from his dean, Jozsef Kovacs. Ordered by phone to the dean's office in Arad on April 1, he found an Inspector for Church Affairs and the dean waiting for him. The dean presented Laszlo with an official document announcing his suspension from his pastorate, the initiation of disciplinary proceedings, and the appointment of Sandor Halasz as Laszlo's successor. The following day was a Sunday. Dean Kovacs and a colleague turned up unannounced at the church in Timisoara. Their mission was to take possession of Laszlo's office and place the congregation under the direct supervision of the dean. Dean Kovacs forbade Laszlo to preach and he took the service himself.

The self-invited "guest preacher" lacked the courage to announce from the pulpit the purpose of his visit. "It was none of the congregation's business," he told Laszlo. But news had already circulated about the scheme to remove Laszlo. Laszlo believed that it was the business of the faithful and had kept them informed of the plot against him and the congregation. The congregation was incensed. Shouts of "We want Laszlo Tokes to preach!" greeted the dean as he addressed the congregation from the pulpit. The believers gave Dean Kovacs an earful as he departed. The congregation was outraged that the Church leaders should try to achieve their dubious purposes in such an underhanded way. The trembling dean left the church with his mission unfulfilled.

Laszlo received determined support from his thriving congregation. The more active and better-educated parishioners well understood the complex issues of church and secular politics that were at the heart of Bishop Papp's persecution of Laszlo. But the simple folk, too, knew that right was on the side of their young pastor. He had passed the simple biblical test: "A tree is recognized by its fruit. . . . The good man brings good things out of the good stored up in him" (Matthew 12:33, 35). Laszlo's fruit was wholesome and nutritious. When he arrived in Timisoara, the congregation was virtually dead. His fruit nourished the congregation, giving it new life. For decades the church members had experienced crucifixion. Now they had a foretaste of the resurrection. The people would stand by their pastor.

The church council acted immediately. That Monday the council held an extraordinary meeting. The members decisively rejected the bishop's suspension order and sent a telegram to the Church authorities, declaring that the congregation would not accept an appointee to replace Laszlo. The resolve of the congregation did not deter the authorities from trying to remove Laszlo. On April 13 the church court of the deanery was summoned by Bishop Papp. It voted to suspend Laszlo and initiate disciplinary proceedings against him. He was accused of "disturbing the life of faith" and "serious violations endangering the peaceful life of the congregation." It was a kangaroo court. Laszlo had not been informed about the hearing and was thus unable to defend himself.

By mid-May, Bishop Papp and his superiors in the Department of Religious Affairs had finalized their plan for Laszlo. He was to be transferred to the remote village of Mineu (Menyo, in Hungarian). Nestled in the hills of the Salaj region of Transylvania, Mineu was virtually cut off from the outside world. The hamlet was accessible only by a single rutted dirt track. Mineu had a quaint wooden Reformed Church but few parishioners. Half of the village's 100 inhabitants were ethnic Romanians.

Sending "turbulent" pastors and priests to such out of the way locations was one of the the regime's preferred methods of silencing troublemakers. Laszlo's bold friend Janos Molnar had ended up serving in such villages. This practice had two advantages for the authorities. On the one hand, it severely limited the influence of the offending cleric. He might shout, but no one would hear. He might work hard to evangelize, but only a few would be affected. On the other hand, it produced far fewer international complications than murder or imprisonment. Moreover, the regime could always pin the blame on the bishop.

During the spring and summer, persistent efforts were made to separate Laszlo from his congregation. Hardly a week went by without Laszlo being summoned to receive a dressing down from some Church official. Sometimes it was Bishop Papp himself. More often than not, it was one of his closest cronies or poor Dean Kovacs, a hapless victim of the corrupt system. Delegations of Church leaders came and went from Timisoara, reissuing transfer or suspension orders and trying to occupy Laszlo's office. They were always rebuffed by Laszlo and his loyal church council.

The regime also became directly involved. Timisoara's Chief Inspector of Church Affairs, Mihai Teperdel, turned up at Laszlo's apartment on April 7. He behaved civilly, unlike some of the Church leaders. The chief inspector told Laszlo that the state viewed the Tokes affair as an internal church dispute. The state would not intervene, he said. But Teperdel advised Laszlo to compromise with Bishop Papp to ensure a peaceful solution to the controversy. He also accused Laszlo of inciting his people to revolt. Teperdel asked Laszlo to "calm down" the congregation.

Laszlo was not fooled by the conciliatory words of the chief inspector. He knew that Bishop Papp did only what the Ceausescu regime commanded. A shamefaced Dean Kovacs soon afterward admitted to Laszlo what he already knew: his public condemnation of the village destruction policy and his zealous youth work were the real reasons for his problems with the Church leadership.

Laszlo had no doubt that cooperation with Teperdel would be a dangerous business and, in all probability, would lead to a trap. Laszlo stuck to his guns. He told Teperdel what he told his ecclesiastical superiors: the suspension and transfer orders were contrary to the constitution of the Reformed Church. The indignation of his congregation was spontaneous. He would remain at his post, serving the faithful and the broader community in accordance with the will of his congregation. Teperdel left dissatisfied but did not give up. The chief inspector thereafter joined the Church leaders as a regular feature of the almost farcical, yet deadly serious, circus of comings and goings at the Reformed Church in Timisoara.

Laszlo and his church council used every legal means at their disposal to combat the attack on their rights. Scores of letters were sent, appeals lodged and petitions presented. All were ignored by the Church leaders. Many were returned unopened. On April 27 the congregation did what Bishop Papp had wished to prevent for the previous two years. It elected Laszlo as its full-time, permanent pastor. Laszlo was no longer officially an assistant pastor under the direct control of the bishop. His legal position in the congregation was now secure.

One month later, the congregation sent an eight-man delegation to call on Bishop Papp in Oradea. Their mission was to present a petition in support of Laszlo. As they boarded the train at Timisoara, they wondered whether their journey would have any effect. They knew the state was behind the bishop's actions. When anyone fought the state, the state always seemed to win.

The delegation went straight from Oradea's train station to the bishop's office. Mounting the stairs, they entered the bishop's stately, spacious rooms. The atmosphere was quiet and studious. Papp's deputy, Jozsef Zsigmond, received them rudely. The bishop was busy and could not see the group, Zsigmond barked. Laszlo's supporters insisted on waiting till the bishop was free. They wanted Papp to see for himself their determination to resist the illegal transfer. Laszlo was their pastor both spiritually and legally. When they refused to leave, Zsigmond flew into a rage. He threatened to call the police to have them removed by force. The bishop and the state were now locked in an unholy alliance. The bishop supported the state against its own people. The state supported the bishop against his own people. Dispirited but not surprised, the delegation finally left to begin the long trek back to Timisoara.

The Net Tightens

Laszlo was not the only one to pay for his defiance. Harassment of Laszlo's father, Istvan, was also stepped up. He was barred from preaching in the Twin Towers church in his hometown of Cluj. He was due to preach on Pentecost Sunday, but a few days earlier the pastor called him in. He told Istvan that the Church leadership had issued instructions that he was not to let Istvan preach. He was also due to preach later at Cluj's Inner City church, but this, too, was cancelled.

The elders of the Twin Towers church had invited the seventy-two-year-old former professor to preach at midweek services and at certain festivals. Now he was barred from the pulpit. Istvan immediately wrote a letter of protest to the Church leadership. He likened the ban on his preaching to "taking away the pen from a writer or the brush from a painter." Since his dismissal as deputy bishop and removal from his teaching post, Istvan had been a constant thorn in the flesh of the Church leaders.

The net around Laszlo was slowly tightening. Papp was furious at his insolence and defiance. The letters of support that Laszlo's congregation had written to Papp only seemed to increase the bishop's determination to oust him. The Securitate was no doubt pressuring Papp to step up his attack.

But Laszlo was determined to resist. When the bishop began legal proceedings to have him removed, Laszlo was able to call on the services of a good friend from his Dej days, Ferenc Ujvari. Ferenc was a lawyer by profession, now retired, with a strong interest in the Church. He helped Laszlo immensely. They both agreed that, where possible, they should resist illegal demands through legal means.

Panorama

Stephen was dispirited but did not despair. Perhaps there would be an interest in the interview in Hungary. Feeling against the anti-Hungarian policies of the Ceausescu regime was already running high. He flew to Budapest in June and made arrangements for the film to be shown to the International Affairs Director of Hungarian Television, Alajos Chrudinak. Chrudinak knew he was onto an exciting scoop. He immediately began preparations for broadcast on the prestigious current affairs program "Panorama."

While harassment continued, Laszlo's long-delayed bombshell was dropped. On July 24, Hungarian television finally broadcast his March interview on the "Panorama" news program. Propped against the benches in the balcony overlooking the church, Laszlo looked cool and determined. Using careful, composed sentences he occasionally reinforced his words with hand gestures to emphasize his points. His low-key, calm delivery, combined with a powerful but restrained argument, moved his viewers.

Laszlo's words had an electrifying effect. Horror and outrage about the village destruction plans had been growing all around the world, but especially in Hungary. People feared this would be the final straw in destroying the Hungarians' separate cultural identity in Transylvania. Laszlo's fearless interview spurred the people into action and made Laszlo a household figure throughout Hungary. It propelled Laszlo from being an obscure fighter for human rights into a world figure.

Hungarian television could be seen in Timisoara, Oradea and other places along the border. People watched these shows avidly while Romanian television showed only a steady diet of Ceausescu's interminable speeches and visits around the country. So many people saw Laszlo's fearless interview for themselves. News quickly traveled farther inland to places where Hungarian TV did not reach. Laszlo's bluntness was a surprise and a source of amazement.

The response of the Romanian authorities was immediate. Laszlo's home was put under twenty-four-hour surveillance at once. Stones were thrown at the windows of the flat. Several times Laszlo's three-year-old son, Mate, was nearly hit by stones and flying glass. Anonymous death threats began. Laszlo dared to go out only in the company of others. He was afraid he would be "kidnapped" and killed.

Laszlo's appearance on "Panorama" coincided with Billy Graham's July, 1989, Hungarian crusade. Both Hungarian and Romanian evangelicals hoped that Dr. Graham would use the occasion to give public support and comfort to the oppressed faithful in Romania, where his words would be heard via Hungarian TV. Three prominent evangelical pastors from Budapest, Geza Nemeth, Gabor Ivanyi and Gyozo Dobner wrote to the evangelist. They asked him to speak out against the widespread and systematic violations of religious liberty in the Communist world, Romania in particular. Hungarian journalists pressed Dr. Graham to show Christian solidarity with the endangered Laszlo Tokes.

Caution prevailed within the Billy Graham team. The evangelist issued vague statements in favor of human rights. To the faithful in Hungary and Romania, such utterances sounded uncomfortably familiar. They sounded like the meaningless platitudes made over the years by their own Communist tyrants for the benefit of Western public opinion. Graham and his advisors had a dilemma. They had big plans for sensational crusades in the Soviet Union and China. Taking up the cause of Tokes and the suffering church in Romania might cause problems. The Soviet and Chinese leaders might not allow the evangelist to have a public platform in their countries, where there was no shortage of embarrassing human rights problems.

Should Billy Graham speak out and run the risk of being prevented from preaching the Gospel of salvation to millions? Or should he play the propaganda game of the Communists, a game long played by the World Council of Churches, in order to gain access to those thirsting for the Gospel behind the Iron Curtain? These were the questions the Graham team was wrestling with during his five-day sojourn in Budapest.

Billy Graham tried to play it safe. When invited to appear on "Panorama" to speak in defense of the hard-pressed Tokes, he said he did not have the time. The Budapest crusade drew record numbers and the response to his invitation to repent was overwhelming. But Billy Graham paid heavily.

The Hungarian press gave him a roasting. Many believers and nonbelievers alike found it hard to reconcile the clear and powerful preaching of repentance with his rather ambiguous utterances about those persecuted for their Christian witness in totalitarian societies.

In the end, the pressure on Graham had its intended effect. Shortly after his departure from Hungary, a brief statement issued by the Billy Graham Association appeared in the Hungarian press: "Billy Graham unambiguously acknowledges the pain of all those who are forced to endure persecution. Billy Graham therefore has great sympathy with Reverend Laszlo Tokes of Temesvar [Timisoara], who, along with others in his company, today are still obliged to endure injustices." The Ceausescu regime was not pleased. Was this its reward for the red carpet treatment given to the evangelist during his 1985 Romanian crusade?

*   *   *

Visitors to Laszlo's home were often subjected to body searches and questioning by the police. The state was determined to isolate this turbulent minister from his people. Some members of his congregation stayed away in the growing climate of fear, but most stood by Laszlo. They came to see him and his family in spite of the harassment this would certainly bring.

Week after week, as the temperature gradually rose, Laszlo's people would gather in the austere church. As he mounted the steep wooden steps to the pulpit each Sunday and gazed down on his flock, he saw the determination in their eyes. They would support him and his fight for independence and freedom. Each week there were new faces, as more and more people came to hear him. His mostly Hungarian flock was joined by Romanians. He began to preach in Romanian as well as Hungarian. Word traveled fast in Timisoara, and Laszlo's courageous stand made him a local hero.

On August 6, Laszlo was taken for questioning by the police. They held him for several hours and asked him all kinds of questions.

The Bishop's Last Gasp

Bishop Papp had reached the end of his tether. He had tried everything in his power to force Laszlo out of Timisoara. But nothing worked. Laszlo and the congregation outsmarted him every time. The Romanian authorities were not pleased with the bishop. They had given him the job of silencing his prophet pastor, hoping to make the Tokes affair appear as no more than the sort of squalid internal squabble that afflicts every church, East or West, from time to time. But the bishop had failed in his mission.

Bishop Papp was granted one last chance to execute his assignment. He convened a meeting of the Timisoara church council on August 13. He asked the members for the last time to reject Laszlo and accept a new pastor. He should have known better. The faithful band unconditionally rejected his proposal. Bishop Papp had no legal grounds for imposing his will on the congregation. Long ago he lost any moral authority to influence the church council's decisions. The following day Bishop Papp and his episcopal colleague from Cluj, Bishop Nagy, issued a joint letter which was sent to all the Reformed congregations in Romania. The bishops established four essential criteria of a good Reformed pastor:

1. All the sermons and statements of a pastor must nurture Christ-like love.
2. A pastor must show respect toward the Church authorities and is obliged to obey their decrees and resolutions.
3. A pastor must act in accordance with the decrees of the government.
4. A pastor must act according to the requirements of the church and the civil authorities.

Bishops Papp and Nagy declared that Laszlo had dismissed himself as pastor of the Reformed Church for failing to live up to these criteria. Laszlo Tokes, they charged, had "violated the laws of the church and the state."

This was an ominous sign. The bishops' statement clearly implied that they no longer had any responsibility for Laszlo. They could now wash their hands of the murky Tokes affair. The Ceausescu regime had had enough of the clumsy efforts of the bishops. The state authorities now came to the fore. They abandoned the fiction that the state was a neutral, disinterested observer of Laszlo's conflict with the Church leadership. Bishop Papp retreated to the background in disgrace, alienated from his flock and despised by his Communist masters.

Not one of the Church's 700 pastors spoke up in Laszlo's defense. Through cowardice or fear they kept their heads down and hoped the whole "Tokes affair" would go away. They knew that, if they spoke up, their days, too, would be numbered. Laszlo was disappointed—but hardly surprised—by this lack of support from his colleagues. Years of living under such a dictatorship had sapped their moral courage. They had grown to accept harassment, restrictions and state control. All they wanted was a quiet life.

Even retired pastors—who had no church to lose—did not dare to speak up: only two signed a letter of protest. One of them was Laszlo's father, Istvan. The open letter gained more support from Transylvanian writers—some of whom rarely went to church—and from a prominent Catholic priest.

Opposition to the state's restrictions had already begun to stir in the Catholic Church. A group of nineteen priests got together to write to their bishop, Antal Jakab. They expressed the fear that, if they did not speak out, they would risk the just accusation of being—in the words of the prophet Isaiah—"dumb dogs." The priests attacked the restrictions on seminary entry, the ban on the building of churches in new housing districts, the almost total ban on church publishing, restrictions on the Bible and the discrimination against Hungarians in Romania. They made their statement public earlier in 1989 when the authorities banned a mass to commemorate the respected Catholic bishop Aron Marton, who died in 1980 after years of imprisonment and house arrest.

But the Reformed Church was different. Laszlo was on his own. This was hardly the time to be protesting in Romania. As anti-Communist forces were gaining ground in other countries of Eastern Europe, Ceausescu was taking no chances. He warmly applauded the Chinese authorities' massacre of peaceful pro-democracy demonstrators in Beijing in June, 1989. This was the way, he implied, he would deal with any similar trouble. As criticism and condemnation of Romania spread around the world, the country became more and more isolated.

It was a depressing prospect for those in Romania, as the political and economic situation got steadily worse. The few brave dissidents, like the dismissed university lecturer Doina Cornea and the poet Mircea Dinescu, were under house arrest or close Securitate control. As democracy was gaining ground elsewhere, Dinescu surveyed the bleak prospect for his country, which he likened to a deep-frozen mammoth. "Who will intervene in Romania?" he asked pitifully. "God does not get involved in politics. I hope I will be forgiven for saying that our daily prayer does not seem to have been heard."

He looked around for possible sources of hope. "The lawyers? They have been reduced to a state of powerlessness. The police? They are trained only to jump on anyone moving on the streets after ten at night, the time all restaurants, cinemas and theaters close. The press? They are merely apostles of the personality cult. The Soviets? Gorbachev is looking at Romania through dark glasses, like Jaruzelski's. The writers? They have been corrupted. The dissidents? There are too few—and yet many."

And what about the church, the first place Dinescu looked to for signs of hope? "Our priests have been forced into becoming trade unionists in cassocks. The 'accidental' deaths of a few troublesome priests, as well as the 'lay' pressure applied by the civilian representatives of the Secu Monastery to the more talkative members of the clergy, have introduced permanent terror into the holy orders. There are no Polish-style Catholic shipyards or factories in our country. There is no militant church, no miracle-working icon like the one in Czestochowa. Our icons are of the president; our factories are run by soldiers; and our churches have, in the winter, the highest number of funerals in the world."

And Dinescu warned, in chilling words that could equally apply to Laszlo: "Once marked as a protester, you must learn to be careful—not to walk alone in town, for instance, or to let your children play outside. You must take care to disinfect your door handle thoroughly; it may be poisoned."

Istvan and Erzsebet Tokes proudly display their family. (Courtesy Jozsef Tokes.)

Istvan conducting Laszlo and Edith's wedding. Dej, December 1985. (Courtesy Jozsef Tokes.)

Revolutionary Cluj, December 1989. (Courtesy Romanian Aid Fund.)

A victim of the revolution. Cluj, December 1989. (Courtesy Romanian Aid Fund.)

Tired but happy: Laszlo after the revolution.

Right: Return to Dej, January 1990.

Below: Arriving for the service in Dej under armed guard.

Janos and Irma Molnar.

With Laszlo Hamos, president of the Hungarian Human Rights Foundation (left) and President George Bush in Oval Office. Visit to United States and Canada, March 1990. (Hungarian Human Rights Foundation.)

In front of the Capitol with the Reverend James D. Ford, chaplain of the United States House of Representatives. (Hungarian Human Rights Foundation.)

Left: Laszlo and Canadian Prime Minister Brian Mulroney. (Hungarian Human Rights Foundation.)

Below: With Senator Christopher Dodd of Connecticut. (Hungarian Human Rights Foundation.)

Left: Presentation of Georgetown University's President's Award by the Reverend Leo Donovan, president of Georgetown University. (Hungarian Human Rights Foundation.)

Below: Interview with John McLaughlin for "One on One" television program. (Hungarian Human Rights Foundation.)

TEN

A Deadly Game

The ring of the usually dormant telephone startled Laszlo. The words he heard were even more alarming. "You will not live to preach next Sunday," announced the anonymous caller, no doubt a member of the secret police. Then the caller raged in disgust that the entire Hungarian population had not been exterminated after the First World War. There would be no Hungarian "problem" today. The agent hung up.

Laszlo's telephone never worked when his friends, relatives and parishioners tried to call. But it mysteriously worked when the Securitate phoned with anonymous death threats. Laszlo tried not to let the increasing atmosphere of violence trouble him. But it was clear that events had taken a dangerous turn since he was declared defrocked by the bishops. The Securitate's surveillance of the church complex was intensified. Laszlo and Edith dared not leave their apartment without a trusted friend or two at their side. Anything might happen. They were becoming virtual prisoners.

The Securitate was cunning. By now they had become convinced of Laszlo's unbreakable resolve and willingness for martyrdom. Moreover, they knew that direct measures against Laszlo would soon become known in the outside world. The Securitate therefore opted for a time-tested tactic: strike the enemy by striking friends and loved ones.

A senior elder of the church, Tibor Unterweiger, was thrown from a trolley car by unknown assailants. The seventy-seven-year-old Unterweiger was later roughed up on the street in broad daylight. Another elder, Istvan Sule, had countless telephone death threats and was often hauled in by the police. During one visit the police raided his home. They said they were looking for currency he had used to buy meat on the black market. Not finding any money, they took away some Bibles. The police agents refused to say what was illegal about owning Bibles.

Another member of the church was attacked in the street by police agents. His right leg was kicked in what seemed a premeditated plan. The following day the agents attacked him again, going to work on his left leg. The kicking was so vicious that his muscles were ruptured.

The danger really came home to Laszlo in mid-September. The Securitate was not playing around. Laszlo's close friend and faithful parishioner Erno Ujvarossy was in serious trouble. Erno, a building engineer by profession, had faithfully stood by his pastor. He had taken part in the church council's fruitless delegation to the office of Bishop Papp and had written letters of protest. Laszlo had always had great affection for Erno. His wife had died in tragic circumstances and his son suffered from a serious illness. He had found solace and support in Laszlo's congregation. He had selflessly given of his time and skills to help restore the church.

As the Securitate increased the pressure on him, Erno's once daily visits to the church became less frequent. Laszlo was worried. When he saw Erno, he seemed dispirited and hardly answered the pastor's questions. He said only that strangers had threatened him with "negative consequences." They said he would be transferred to a job in Cernavoda, a town on the other side of the country, near the Black Sea. His son, they also warned, would lose his job. As a conscientious pastor, Laszlo felt an obligation to try to help his friend. But what could he do? Should he yield to the dark powers and leave his congregation?

Erno disappeared from his home on Tuesday, September 12. By Friday no news had been heard of him. Laszlo was so concerned that he wrote to Bishop Papp. Laszlo told Papp that Erno had become increasingly dispirited and afraid as attempts were made to drive a wedge between members of the congregation and their pastor. Laszlo blamed Papp for this and called on him to help find Ujvarossy.

Laszlo and his friends heard nothing until September 16. Then they were told that a police patrol had found Erno's body in some woods near Timisoara two days earlier. He was found lying on some dead leaves in his own blood, his face badly bruised. The postmortem declared he had died of poisoning from his own medicines. Was this true? Maybe the authorities were right when they said he had committed suicide—enough terror was being imposed by the secret police. Whether they murdered him or forced him into suicide, everyone knew the state would now stop at nothing.

The death chilled members of the congregation. The secret police had deliberately picked on one of the weakest and most vulnerable members of the church. Who would be next?

Laszlo had a heavy heart as he conducted the funeral service for Erno the following Monday. But he was determined to encourage the faithful, even in this dark hour. This was the first time Laszlo had been outside the church complex for some days. As the car taking him to the cemetery pulled away, another car pulled out behind it. He was constantly being watched.

Only about thirty people attended the funeral—the rest were too frightened. As mourners arrived at the graveyard, two men took photographs of them. The Securitate had infiltrated the funeral. Laszlo's friend Zoltan Balaton arrived late at the graveside, and a Securitate camera clicked in his face. Zoltan's spine tingled with fear. But he and the other mourners refused to be intimidated.

Laszlo read a psalm, then led the mourners in a traditional Hungarian ballad. The folk song was about twelve builders constructing a fortress. The mourners immediately knew why Laszlo chose this ballad. Erno had spent long hours carrying out major repairs on the church. Each time the twelve built an edifice, so went the ballad, it was immediately destroyed. And with each demolition the twelve faithful builders started to rebuild. Finally the twelve decided the first of the builders' wives to arrive would be killed and her body built into the fortress to protect it. She would be sacrificed to protect the building. The message of this grim tale was clear to all. Laszlo spoke powerfully on the theme of sacrifice. God's fortress cannot be built without sacrifice. The community would become stronger.

After Erno's funeral, the elders and members of the congregation were systematically harassed by the Securitate. They were called in one by one to government security bureaus and intimidated. The Securitate used psychological pressure to "persuade" the parishioners to fire Laszlo. The same tactic was used on the parishioners as was used on Laszlo. If they failed to comply, the security agents warned, loved ones would suffer. A highly talented daughter would never get to the university. A spouse would be sent to work in a remote part of the country. A son would lose his job.

On September 30, the chairman of the council of elders and one of its members were summoned to the Communist Party headquarters of Timisoara County. They were told that, if the council did not fire Laszlo, the church would be closed down and every elder would be fined 5,000 lci, roughly the equivalent of one month's salary.

A high-ranking official of the Department of Religious Affairs in Bucharest turned up in Timisoara on October 4. After consulting with local officials, he called at Laszlo's apartment. Let's make a deal, he offered. You give up the congregation and we will give you "safe passage" out of Romania. The official hoped Laszlo would be tempted to abandon his post by the possibility of emigrating to the West. Laszlo could imagine how nice it would be to minister to a congregation freely, to sleep at night without fear, to have a spacious house and two cars.

But Laszlo would not take the bait. He could not trust the authorities to keep any promise of safe passage. But, more importantly, Laszlo was determined to stay in Transylvania. The authorities might succeed in ousting him from his church, he thought, but they would never force him to leave his homeland. For Laszlo, serving the people in Transylvania was a sacred trust. He would remain with them through thick and thin.

Calling Their Bluff

Undeterred by Laszlo's unwillingness to cooperate, the Bucharest official ordered the chairman of the council of elders to appear before him on the following day. He demanded that the council come together that evening to dismiss Laszlo. If the council failed to comply, he threatened, the church would be closed within two days. The dismissal of Laszlo by the council of elders was important to the authorities. Some months earlier the local Chief Inspector for Church Affairs, Mihai Teperdel, and Bishop Papp had jointly initiated legal proceedings to evict Laszlo from his apartment in the church complex. The authorities wanted to be able to show the world that the elders had fired Laszlo. Then, they reasoned, Laszlo would have no defense in court.

Laszlo and the elders called the officials' bluff. Sunday services were held as usual on October 8. It was one thing to ignore the huffing and puffing of Bishop Papp but quite another to disobey the commands of the government officials. More force was required. On Saturday,

October 14, the Securitate tried to convene an elders' meeting. A letter from Bishop Papp was sent to all thirty-one elders, inviting them to an extraordinary meeting in the pastor's office. Most of the elders were immediately suspicious. Why hadn't Laszlo called them to the meeting? Only five showed up. Securitate agents then swooped in on the homes and workplaces of the rest, but only three others could be found. They were taken by force to the church.

With only eight of the thirty-one elders present, the authorities failed to achieve a quorum. Laszlo kept the door of his office locked, so the eight intimidated elders and their Securitate minders held their farcical meeting in the corridor. The eight were forced to vote for Laszlo's suspension. Laszlo and the congregation gave no credence to this "decision" of the rump council. Fifteen hundred members and friends of the congregation had already signed a petition in support of their pastor. Laszlo prepared for the Sunday service as usual.

On Sunday morning the police blocked off the streets surrounding the church. They hoped a large police presence would frighten away the overflow crowds that now came to hear Laszlo preach. Policemen entered the church and stood guard outside the door of his apartment. But Laszlo had anticipated this move and had already left for a hiding place near the sanctuary. The police were dumbfounded when they saw Laszlo enter the sanctuary in his black clerical robe to a standing ovation. The church was packed. A government official rose and began to harangue the congregation. The faithful hooted him down before he had uttered more than a few words.

The service continued. The congregation had scored another victory.

After the rump council meeting and the attempt to physically prevent him from preaching that weekend, Laszlo wrote to President Ceausescu to complain about the persecution. He requested an investigation into the attacks on him and his congregation. He would not let himself be cowed into silence. If the world forgot him, he would be destroyed. Laszlo kept up his stream of statements, protests and open letters.

Within a week of the turbulent church service, the eviction proceedings against Tokes reached the civil court. Laszlo dared not appear for fear of being prevented from returning to his home. He was represented by his lawyer and supported in the gallery by a few friends. The court found in favor of the plaintiffs. It agreed that Laszlo was no longer legally a minister of the Reformed Church and had no right to live in the pastor's apartment. He was granted five days in which to appeal against the ruling. He filed his appeal within the time limit.

The violence surrounding Laszlo did not abate. Bela Sepsi, the husband of one of the church's elders, had continued to support Laszlo publicly. Now persecution was stepped up at his workplace. Bela was a driver, and the authorities threatened to move him to another job. In the Socialist Republic of Romania, the regime held all the cards: they controlled where people worked, where they lived and even, through the system of ration cards, what they could eat.

Then they plotted a case against Bela. They planted 300 German marks behind a map on the wall of his house. Then the secret police came in, immediately "discovering" the money. They accused him of illegal possession of foreign currency. Bela had a stroke and was taken to the intensive care unit of Timisoara Central Hospital. He spent several months in a coma.

Laszlo made a vain attempt to gain the support of the local Orthodox bishop, Metropolitan Nicolae Corneanu. He wrote a letter on October 17 describing what he termed the authorities' "merciless campaign" against himself and his congregation. He mentioned the house searches, persecution and threats by the authorities, the police and the Securitate against members of the church. In a spirit of genuine ecumenism, Laszlo called on Metropolitan Nicolae to lend his support.

Ten days later, he received a very dusty answer from the bishop, who attacked Laszlo's stories of harassment and persecution as "tendentious and slanderous" and said that, in his forty years in Timisoara, he had known no one who had caused as much damage to relations between different nationalities and the churches as Laszlo. He called on Laszlo's honor, "if you have such a thing," and on his conscience, "if it still functions," to reconsider his position. Laszlo hardly expected Metropolitan Nicolae to support him unequivocally, but he was disappointed by the cowardly answer.

On October 23, Zoltan Balaton and Lajos Varga, two key friends of Laszlo from the congregation, were banished from Timisoara for a month. The Securitate ordered their workplace to send them out of Transylvania to the distant town of Galati. Back in September, the secret police had discovered the important support they were giving Laszlo. The two knew their "work" in Galati was invented, but there was nothing they could do but comply.

That same day a Reformed seminarian from Cluj disappeared. Istvan Kiss Lukacs was on his way to see his girlfriend in the village of Vargyas. He was never seen alive again. Exactly a month after his disappearance, his family received a package containing his identity card and belongings. Only then did the police inform them of his death. His body—they said—had been found next to a railroad miles away in Buzau. A witness—they told the family—saw him throw himself under a train.

The Catholic Cabbie

As the Ceausescu regime tightened the screws on Laszlo and the Timisoara congregation, his lines of communication with the outside world became increasingly important. If Laszlo was to succeed in resisting the dark power ranged against him, he knew that the foreign media had to be kept informed. This was no simple task with the Securitate mounting a twenty-four-hour surveillance around the church complex.

Laszlo's main lifeline to the world outside was a taxi driver from Budapest, Miklos Kovacs. Miklos was no ordinary cabbie. He became interested in Transylvania back in 1972. He was then a young seminarian studying for the Catholic priesthood at Esztergom in Hungary. He was very curious about the strange land to the east of Hungary because it was almost a taboo subject in Hungarian schools, books and newspapers. The Hungarian Communist authorities were afraid that public discussion of the once-Hungarian Crown Land would offend its

Warsaw Pact ally Romania. Miklos knew that large numbers of ethnic Hungarians continued to live in Transylvania under difficult circumstances. The youthful ordinand felt called to help.

During his summer vacation in 1972, Miklos boarded a train bound for Transylvania. His mission: to deliver important documents of the Second Vatican Council to Bishop Aron Marton of Alba Iulia. Bishop Marton had spent long years in prison and under house arrest for refusing to knuckle under to the Communist authorities. The Romanian government prevented him from representing his church at Vatican II, which was intended to initiate renewal in the Catholic Church. The authorities also banned Vatican II literature from the country. They wished to keep the Catholic Church in isolation to prevent spiritual revival among Romania's 1.3 million Catholics.

Miklos reached Alba Iulia and handed his precious packets over to the grateful bishop. Miklos then headed for the small town of Szepsiszentgyorgy by car with one of Bishop Marton's young priests, Father Laszlo Marton. Well out of Alba Iulia, Miklos and Father Laszlo encountered a common hazard of enemies of the Ceausescu regime. A car suddenly came from nowhere, crashing into theirs. Father Laszlo was dead. Miklos was severely injured on the head and arm.

Miklos's trip to Transylvania came to an untimely end. But it was not to be his last. Miklos felt he had a calling to return. Within months, he was back distributing banned Catholic literature to isolated priests. Miklos even got his fellow seminarians at Esztergom involved. Within a few years, twenty-five fellow students were helping eagerly. Bishop Laszlo Lekai, the future Primate of Hungary, even gave Miklos a small sum of money from his own pocket to support the work. But this was a dangerous enterprise, not only in Romania but also in Hungary. It was illegal activity in the eyes of the Hungarian government, which at that time dared not stray far from orthodox Communism.

In 1974, the Romanian police uncovered Miklos's network at the border. The seminarians were hustled off the train and their sacred writings were unceremoniously cast to the ground before their eyes. Romanian and Hungarian police were in cahoots in those days. The Hungarian authorities obliged their Romanian colleagues by depriving the seminarians of their passports, preventing them from leaving the country. They also pressured the Catholic hierarchy to make an example of Miklos. He was summoned into the office of the seminary's rector, Father Laszlo Paskai, later to become head of the Hungarian Catholic Church. There he was informed of his expulsion from the seminary.

Miklos was not deterred by the car crash, nor was he put off by the expulsion. But without a passport, travel to Romania was impossible. He worked as a printer and married. But in the early 1980s, Miklos made a fateful decision. The Hungarian government had broken the norms of socialism by allowing private taxis to compete with the state cab companies. The enterprising Miklos took up the challenge and went into business for himself. Then in 1987, one of Miklos's customers, a Catholic lady of Hungarian origin from Toronto, asked Miklos if he would transport food, medicine, Christian literature and clothes to the faithful in Transylvania.

Miklos could not refuse. Here was his chance to resume the work he had begun in his youth. By now his name was off the Hungarians' passport blacklist. In fact, the Hungarian authorities were beginning to turn a blind eye to organized efforts to support the Hungarians in Transylvania. Miklos established a network of co-workers to send the aid received from Canada to the long-suffering church folk in Transylvania. The Romanian frontier was hard to penetrate. Border guards customarily made travelers from Hungary wait hours and subjected them to humiliating searches before allowing them to enter the country. Out of every ten cars sent by Miklos, three or four would have their cargo discovered and confiscated.

Miklos was a fairly conservative Catholic and had few Protestant contacts in Transylvania. But one of his Catholic friends from eastern Hungary was related by marriage to the Tokes family. Miklos began transporting medicine to Laszlo's sister Anna, who was a doctor. Anna directed Miklos to Laszlo in Timisoara. The two met for the first time in September, 1988, when Laszlo was in trouble for the memorandum against village destruction. It was a fateful meeting.

Miklos the Catholic and Laszlo the Calvinist became friends. It was too dangerous for Miklos to visit Laszlo personally on a regular basis. But he made sure that Laszlo was visited frequently by other drivers. Laszlo never failed to give messages to Miklos's couriers. Sometimes they received hastily recorded tapes, other times messages on paper. Miklos and his drivers were masters of smuggling messages out of Romania. They were all intimately familiar with the routine at the border. But they had problems after the Securitate intensified its surveillance of Laszlo. If a courier turned up on a Sunday, a tape or envelope could be handed over during the service without attracting the attention of the police. During weekdays, the messages sometimes had to be thrown out of a window and picked up in the church courtyard by a child companion of the courier.

Once the messages reached Budapest, Miklos would disseminate news to the press. The secular media in Hungary devoured the news. Christian press services and human rights organizations in the West, such as Christian Solidarity International, The Hungarian Human Rights Foundation, Glaube in der Zweiten Welt, and Keston College, did much to make the case of Laszlo Tokes known. But they had the same experience as Laszlo's brother Stephen and his Canadian film crew. The major organs of the Western media still did not show much interest in the fate of the young unknown pastor in Timisoara.

Father and Son

Saturday, October 28. Istvan was preparing to leave Cluj for Timisoara. Ignoring his bishop's ban on preaching, he was determined to show solidarity with his besieged son by proclaiming the Word at the Reformation Day service in Timisoara, October 31. With his sixteen-year-old granddaughter as a companion, Istvan set off for the station to catch the afternoon express train.

The journey to Timisoara took seven hours. Arriving at 9:30 P.M., the two weary travelers made the steep dismount from the train. Uniformed police and Securitate suddenly appeared and took them to police rooms at the train station for interrogation. "What are you doing in Timisoara?" "Who are you going to visit?" "Where did you get your money?" So the questioning went. The officers accused Istvan of coming there to engage in black marketeering. They informed him that Laszlo no longer lived in Timisoara.

There was no news of Istvan and his granddaughter. Laszlo was getting worried. Where could they be? Not a word of their whereabouts had reached the family. Would his enemies really pick on a seventy-two-year-old man and a sixteen-year-old girl?

The two were held all night, sitting on a bench in a cold, unheated room. No one, either in Cluj or in Timisoara, was told where they were being held. The next day two uniformed policemen escorted Istvan and his granddaughter back to Cluj on the train. When they arrived, the policeman told the station officials never to sell Istvan a ticket again.

Laszlo was desperately trying to find out what had happened to them. He had been expecting them to arrive on Saturday evening, but there had been no word. Finally, on Monday evening, he was able to get through to Cluj on the phone. Just as he started speaking to Istvan, the line was cut. "What kind of a country is this where a father can't even talk to his own son?" Istvan asked in anger.

On Tuesday evening, Laszlo held the traditional Reformation Day service. He was following an old tradition. His fellow pastors had followed state pressure—and the specific order of Bishop Papp—to downplay the day and exclude young people from participation in the service. Because of all the trouble the previous year with the drama group, Laszlo did not want to bring more trouble on the youth. So he fulfilled a long-standing ambition to invite some famous actors from as far afield as Cluj and Tirgu Mures to take part in the service. Laszlo had to proceed without his father as guest preacher.

Laszlo had a sense of foreboding that this week would be his last. Perhaps they would break in and drag him away. The council of elders had almost ceased to function—fear was spreading.

Only the brave ones even dared to come to church now. But the life of the community was continuing. More and more people came to the services and the church was always full.

Attack

A few bold friends visited Laszlo and Edith on the Thursday evening after the Reformation Day service. The Tokeses thrived on the company of their good friends. Without their companionship, survival would have been even more difficult. After a few hours of rare relaxation, all the visitors but one couple bid Laszlo and Edith good night. The remaining foursome continued their conversation in the sun parlor. All was quiet. It was half-past seven. Edith went out for a moment. She thought she heard something suspicious.

No sooner had she returned to the sun parlor than the front door crashed in. Four men wearing stocking masks stood there. Screaming inarticulately, they lunged at Laszlo and his guests. Two of them started slashing with knives. Mate hid behind a glass door, watching in horror as the four intruders hit, kicked and wrestled. Chairs and tables were overturned, glasses and china smashed.

The four masked men had obviously not expected the visitors. They tried to surround Laszlo, but he escaped and ran for a side door. Edith grabbed Mate and fled to the windows overlooking the street. Two of the thugs were grappling with Laszlo's visitors, the third was watching the way out. The fourth ran after Laszlo, brandishing a knife. He gashed him on the forehead. Laszlo grabbed a chair and started hitting the man on the wrist, trying to dislodge the knife. The knife fell spinning to the floor as the man fell to the ground. Laszlo kicked the weapon out of reach.

The other three attackers were getting nervous. They kept looking behind them at the door, as if in fear of being disturbed. They signaled to leave. The other man scrambled to his feet and they fled. They took nothing.

The whole incident lasted two minutes. Not one word had been exchanged with the intruders. As Laszlo and the others caught their breath they thought about what might have happened. Laszlo rushed to his pregnant wife. She had slumped exhausted into a chair. Mate was still gazing wide-eyed in disbelieving horror.

Laszlo knew that it was the unexpected presence of their visitors that had saved them. Without them, they would be dead. People would suspect the authorities, but without witnesses, who could say for sure? Now the only question was: When would the men return?

The authorities had cut off Laszlo's telephone three months before, so the visiting couple had to go to the neighbors to phone the police. The police called the Securitate: they knew the case was sensitive. They arrived together.

These agents of "law and order" feigned surprise that

Laszlo's phone was not working. They claimed to be mystified by the attack. The plainclothes police, who identified, searched and followed every visitor to Laszlo's front door, pretended to have seen nothing unusual. First, the "investigators" blamed it on unknown burglars. Then they accused Laszlo and his friends of staging the incident themselves to win international sympathy. Thus the investigation into the armed attack ended.

Neighbors later told Laszlo they had seen four suspicious-looking men hanging around outside the door for hours. Many people had noticed them in the busy street. The four men had waited until they thought Laszlo's last guests had gone. They hoped to catch Laszlo, Edith and young Mate alone. Laszlo's neighbors knew it was a risky business to inquire too closely about suspicious loiterers, especially directly outside the home of Timisoara's leading "troublemaker."

The terror campaign against the Tokes family continued. It was 7:00 P.M. and pitch-black outside. Suddenly the windows exploded with a crash in Mate's room. Crash followed crash as windows in the church above were shattered. Someone phoned the police. The investigators were unconcerned. They said it was only some innocent children playing with a ball.

Laszlo had to protect himself and his family. Mate was sent to Edith's parents in Dej. Laszlo boarded up the windows with an old door and wooden planks. Iron bars were inserted behind the doors. Barriers went up inside the church complex to obstruct the entry of unwanted intruders from the rear. Laszlo and Edith barricaded themselves in. The church complex became their fortress. Laszlo thought of the immortal words of Martin Luther:

"A mighty fortress is our God, a bulwark never failing!" Laszlo took comfort. Though besieged by a host of dark powers, Laszlo and Edith had a Protector. Laszlo did not know whether God would lead them to triumph or martyrdom. But he was determined to continue his life-or-death struggle to the very end.

As the physical intimidation of Laszlo and Edith failed, the authorities returned to more subtle forms of pressure. They threatened Laszlo with imprisonment for being a foreign agent paid by the West to betray Romania. They said he would spend fifteen years in prison. The fraud squad hauled him away for interrogation, accusing him of embezzling money. They threatened imprisonment of seven or eight years but offered to drop all the fraud charges against him if he helped them solve the "Timisoara problem."

Defying King Herod

Laszlo's most powerful weapon was openness. The agents of the Ceausescu regime operated in darkness. Laszlo revealed everything in the light. At the end of each service—when the announcements for the week were given—he spoke about everything that had happened the previous week. He kept nothing secret. He declared from the pulpit that he had been accused of being a spy and of embezzling money. He told his people of how he was being pressured to collaborate and how the authorities were trying to destroy his will to resist.

The congregation could hardly believe its ears. They well knew the brutal and devious methods of the authorities, but to hear someone expose them in public was astonishing. The underworld of the police and Securitate was a taboo subject. If someone was interrogated or had to go to the police on some routine business, it was not spoken of outside the circle of the family and the most intimate friends. Any kind of contact with the police aroused suspicion that you might be an informer or a dangerous troublemaker. Laszlo believed that what was happening was the business of the congregation and that everyone ought to know.

Sunday after Sunday, Laszlo returned to the pulpit to preach. More and more people came to Sunday services. Ethnic Romanians came, too, and Laszlo would address them in Romanian—a rare sound in a Hungarian Reformed Church. Many people with no church background started to attend, especially students. They were hearing the Gospel for the first time. Laszlo's preaching was relevant. He spoke to the real concerns of the people. In one stirring Advent sermon, he preached on the story of King Herod:

> Herod did not want to believe his ears when, after several days of toings and froings in the palace and the prevarications of troubled courtiers, the news of the Christmas commotion at Bethlehem finally reached him. Hearing, he lost his head. He did so not as a ruler anxious about the fate of his country, or as a tyrant made to tremble by the anger of his people, but like a romancer unpleasantly disturbed in the crazy dream of his glory. His quiet dementia, like stagnant waters whipped up by a storm, turned into enraged raving. He could not sense the danger that threatened his rule. . . .

The connection between the vain and myopic King Herod and the Grand Conducator Nicolae Ceausescu was immediate in the minds of the congregation. Never before had the people heard such prophetic words, at least not before Laszlo arrived in Timisoara.

The authorities tried to cut Laszlo off from all visitors. The guards at the main doors of the building quizzed everyone who wanted to enter. At first they let in only those who had come to arrange a baptism or a burial. Visitors were searched going in and out. Later, all those saying they had come to see Laszlo were turned away. The police even sent away a truck bringing wood for Laszlo's stove. There was nothing to heat his apartment or the church. As winter drew on and the weather got colder, Laszlo's congregation had to smuggle in food and fuel for him under their coats when they came for the Sunday service. They left their parcels under the benches for Laszlo to collect later.

Barricaded in his home, Laszlo was not completely isolated from the world. He could still reach the sanctuary from his apartment. His faithful congregation still came. Miklos's couriers from Hungary still managed to visit him via the church. Guards were posted on the main doors of the building, but visitors could still shin over the wall of the rat-infested yard in back. It was a ten-foot climb, but children from the other apartments would often help Laszlo's secret visitors. Sometimes they kicked messages over the wall attached to soccer balls. The news was brought back to Hungary—at risk to the couriers—where it was immediately published.

Laszlo was protected by the publicity at home and abroad. The Securitate did not know what to do. They had attempted to murder him. They had harassed his congregation. They had tried to banish him. They had physically attacked members of his congregation. They had caused the death of one. Now they were trying to imprison him.

Changing Times

Changes afoot all over Eastern Europe failed to touch Romania. Tadeusz Mazowiecki's appointment as Poland's prime minister on August 24 (the first non-Communist prime minister in the Eastern bloc); the opening of the Berlin Wall on November 8; the huge demonstrations for democracy in Czechoslovakia and Bulgaria in November—Ceausescu would have none of that. Especially worrying for him was the ousting of the old, hardline leaders: Erich Honecker in East Germany, Todor Zhivkov in Bulgaria, Milos Jakes in Czechoslovakia.

The official media kept reminding the Romanian people of what their ally China had done to crush the demonstrators in Tiananmen Square. Addressing the Communist Party congress in November, Ceausescu declared that Eastern Europe's reforms must not, would not happen here. Reform would happen in Romania, he said scornfully, when pears began to grow on apple trees. The party faithful applauded. The Conducator seemed invincible. The orchestrated party congress gave him sixty-seven standing ovations.

Support from Hungarians and Romanians cheered Laszlo and encouraged him. Ninety-nine percent of Hungarians in Transylvania supported him, he believed.

News was reaching him of demonstrations in his support outside the Romanian embassy in Budapest. As a sign of its support, the Hungarian parliament voted on a resolution that Laszlo Tokes and Doina Cornea should be jointly awarded the Nobel peace prize. Even the church press in Hungary was now publicly supporting him. Throughout Hungary, people were thinking of and praying for Laszlo Tokes. This nourished his hope that the authorities could not destroy him under the watchful gaze of the world. He had broken the isolation the Romanian government had tried to put around its citizens.

On December 8, Laszlo addressed a moving letter to Tamas Raj, a prominent rabbi in Hungary. He likened the situation of the Hungarians in Romania to that of the Jews—a persecuted nation for whom the whole world had a duty to raise its voice. Laszlo had always maintained close relations with Erno Neumann, the local rabbi in Timisoara, and the Jewish congregation. However, he had failed in his attempts to gain support from the national Jewish leadership in Romania and especially the Chief Rabbi Moses Rosen. Laszlo called on Raj to lend his support.

Laszlo's letter was smuggled out of Romania and reached Tamas Raj in Budapest late one night. He replied through the pages of the national newspaper, *Magyar Nemzet,* offering comfort to Laszlo through the words of Isaiah: " 'Watchman, what is left of the night?' The watchman replies, 'Morning is coming . . .' " (Isaiah 21:11, 12).

Raj apologized for the hostility shown by his Romanian colleague, the Chief Rabbi Moses Rosen. "The truth is that persecution often debases the persecutor, too," he wrote. Raj recalled his own persecution at the hands of the Hungarian government. And he reminded Laszlo of the words of the Psalmist: "They cried to you and were saved; in you they trusted and were not disappointed" (Psalm 22:5).

Laszlo's friend Zoltan Balaton, a leading member of Laszlo's congregation, was hauled in by the Securitate on December 2. He was told by a senior officer: "We will remove Laszlo Tokes from here and all of you will disappear." In the middle of December, the Securitate began compiling a list of those who would be "liquidated" in Timisoara after Laszlo had been taken away. Of the forty or so names on the list, about thirty were members of Laszlo's church.

On Thursday, December 7, the court in Timisoara announced that Laszlo and his family had to leave their apartment by the 15th of the month. Neither he nor Edith were present. The hearing was over in five minutes. Laszlo had lost his appeal.

Laszlo had no intention of complying with the court ruling. The house belonged to the church congregation. Neither the bishop nor the court had the power to remove him. He was elected by the congregation to be their pastor. They wanted him to stay.

That Sunday he gave the congregation his by now regular update on everything that had happened in the past week. He told them of the court decision. He knew that things were coming to a head. He knew the authorities would move in and evict him by force. Wilder fears flashed through his mind. What would they do to him and his family when they dragged him away?

He calmly asked his people to come and witness the eviction.

And that was when the storm broke. Two hundred people were gathered outside the church on Friday the 15th. That number swelled in the next day and a half, despite threats by Securitate agents and promises from the mayor. By Saturday night, there were thousands of demonstrators. Authorities tried to put down the protest with guns and tanks.

Laszlo and Edith Tokes waited with six friends in their home. At 3:00 A.M., Sunday the 17th, their "eviction" finally came with a crash. Carried off by car to the remote village of Mineu, they waited for their uncertain future to unfold.

ELEVEN

The Demise of the Dictator

Tuesday, December 19. An unmarked car inched through the mud and stopped in front of the pastor's house in Mineu. Laszlo and Edith were returning from their first frightening day of interrogation. The weak and disheveled couple stumbled out of the car into the mire. Armed guards accompanied them through the barbed wire fence to the door of their dwelling.

The house was tidier than when they left in the morning. Women from the congregation had been allowed in to clean and sort out the great pile of belongings from Timisoara that had been dumped there. Laszlo and Edith slumped into chairs for a few moments to regain strength. The strain on the pregnant Edith was almost intolerable, but she was holding her own.

Laszlo carefully switched on the concealed radio. He heard depressing news. The army and Securitate had massacred thousands in Timisoara, according to unconfirmed reports. Laszlo wondered about the fate of his friends and supporters. But there was hope. The regime had not fully regained control of Timisoara and the uprising had spread to other Transylvanian towns: Arad, Brasov and Oradea. He heard conflicting reports about his fate. Some said he and Edith had been shot by the Securitate forces that stormed the church. Others said he had been taken to Moldavia in northeast Romania. Still others said he was now in Mineu.

But Laszlo was heartened by reports of support from around the world, especially Hungary. He was not forgotten. Many were praying for his safety.

On Wednesday, Laszlo listened to the radio again—this time at the interrogation center in Zalau. His inquisitors wanted to hear a speech by the Grand Conducator himself, who had just returned to Romania from an official visit to Iran. The interrogators expected tough words from their hard-line leader. Perhaps hearing the fiery oratory of the dictator himself would weaken Laszlo's resolve, they thought. Laszlo and his captors gathered around the radio.

Laszlo's flesh began to creep when the tyrant spoke about the uprising in Timisoara: "One can say with full conviction that these actions of a terrorist nature were organized and unleashed in close connection with reactionary, imperialistic, irredentist, chauvinist circles and foreign espionage services in various foreign countries. The purpose of these provocative anti-national actions was to provoke disorder, to destabilize the political and economic situation, to create conditions for Romania's dismemberment, and to destroy the independence and sovereignty of our socialist homeland. It was no coincidence that, during these anti-national and terrorist actions, the radio stations in Budapest and other countries had already launched a shameful campaign of slander and lies against our country. . . ." On and on the angry dictator raged.

Laszlo now realized that the authorities were preparing him and the world for a massive show trial. Ceausescu's speech had laid the groundwork for formal charges of treason and espionage. Laszlo's blood ran cold as images of his trial and execution raced through his weary mind.

Narrow Mind

The Grand Conducator was disgusted. Everything had seemed to be in good order when he left Bucharest the previous weekend for his meetings in Iran with the Ayatollahs. The uprising in Timisoara was then still in its infancy. How could it have gotten out of hand? The security forces certainly had the means to quickly crush the revolt. Nicolae had left his loyal and determined wife, Elena, in charge. The President could see no reason Elena and the Securitate chiefs should have had difficulty applying a short, sharp shock to bring the demonstrations to an end. This is what the Communist Party's ruling Politburo had ordered December 17 in response to the events in Timisoara.

Ceausescu's narrow mind could not comprehend that patriotic Romanians might momentarily set aside long-standing differences with Hungarians—differences cunningly exacerbated by his own cynical divide-and-rule policy—to confront his regime. That the forces of law and order should be unable to stamp out the trouble was even more unimaginable. The President suspected treachery within his own ranks. The Securitate began an investigation.

Ceausescu was desperate to show the world and his people that he was firmly in control. He gave orders for the preparation of a huge, nationally televised, pro-government demonstration in Republic Square at noon on Thursday the 21st. And now, as the dictator peered over the balcony of the Central Committee building, he saw a familiar, comforting sight: tens of thousands of people with pro-Communist banners gazing at their leader. The crowd had been bussed in for the rally by workplace Communist Party commissars. Nonattendance could cost you your job. Ceausescu instinctively smiled and waved his arms above his head as he had done at countless political rallies in the past. But this rally was different.

Bucharest, noon, Thursday, December 21. The Grand Conducator announced an across-the-board pay raise to all workers. A women shrieked. Others joined in.

"Killer!"

"Remember Timisoara!" a group of students and workers shouted. Ceausescu smiled and waved again. Perhaps the shouts were accolades from his adoring people. He pressed on with his speech. The shouts and chants grew louder and more threatening. Groups of students and workers began to tear down the picture posters of Ceausescu that adorned the square.

The once-omnipotent dictator began to look bewildered and vulnerable as he perceived the nasty mood of the crowd. The TV cameras kept rolling. Two bodyguards intervened, pulling the President back into the building. Millions witnessed Ceausescu's humiliation before the broadcast came to an abrupt end. The whole country now knew that the tyrant was on the run.

Helicopters flew over the crowds as tanks hemmed the people in. Police wearing helmets and carrying shields fired tear gas into the crowd. Shots were fired as the tanks moved in. Panic-stricken people hid in doorways. Braver souls remained, chanting "Freedom!" and "Down with the dictatorship!" It took two hours to clear the square.

The spirit of Timisoara had finally reached and animated Bucharest, the capital. By mid-afternoon a large crowd had gathered outside the Inter-Continental Hotel. Once hopeless and downtrodden, the people of Bucharest had lost all fear. "Down with Communism," they shouted. "Ceausescu, the criminal!" Helicopters appeared overhead, dropping hastily printed leaflets calling on the people to protect Ceausescu and his socialist achievements. "Fight the troublemakers!" the pamphlets exhorted. Tanks skirted the crowd, obstructed by a barricade of parked trucks. Securitate agents in plainclothes moved through the crowd, trying to provoke violence. They took photos of demonstrators.

Fire engines arrived. Hoses drenched the crowds. The security forces lined the streets in three rows. Boxes of bullets stood on the pavement by the troops. The crowd talked excitedly and listened to speeches. It seemed to be a stalemate. No one seemed to know what to do—neither the demonstrators nor the police. The demonstrators talked earnestly to the soldiers, urging them to join the protests. Some gave them flowers. Some of the soldiers, drafted soldiers only eighteen or nineteen years old, began to cry. The special troops refused to talk, telling the people to go away.

About 5:00 P.M. the shots were fired. People ran in panic. Others stood where they were, prepared now to die. A tank tried to break through the wall of trucks. One truck was set on fire by the demonstrators. For the rest of the evening, small groups roamed the streets shouting anti-government slogans and spreading news of events in Republic Square.

By mid-evening 10,000 people, mainly students and young workers, milled around University Square in the unseasonably warm temperatures. They knew no fear. Student leaders asked the workers to call a general strike. At 10:30 P.M., security forces showered bullets on the youthful anti-Ceausescu demonstrators. The shooting was indiscriminate. Most of the dead and wounded were shot in the back as they fled the carnage. Red lights lit the sky. Shooting continued for more than an hour as the authorities mounted a bloody mop-up operation. Bodies were tossed into trucks and dumped in mass graves on the outskirts of town. The streets of Bucharest were bloodstained. By the early hours of the morning, an eerie silence hung over the capital.

Friday morning, December 22. Unintimidated by the previous night's violence, crowds again assembled at University Square this morning. Army tanks and armored personnel carriers surrounded the Square. This time the Securitate forces were nowhere to be seen. Suddenly a soldier stood up in one of the tanks and emptied the ammunition from his rifle. The crowd watched, bewildered.

Other soldiers followed suit. "The army is with us!" cried the students. Young people climbed the tanks and shoved Christmas tree branches down the gun barrels. Soldiers and students hugged each other. The crowd and groups of soldiers proceeded from University Square to the Communist Party headquarters.

The Tyrant Flees

Ceausescu and his advisors were outraged. How could the carefully planned pro-government demonstration go so radically wrong? Why was security in the capital so disorganized? Why were some army troops reluctant to fire? Who was sabotaging their efforts to regain control of the country? Ceausescu's investigators had an answer: the Defense Minister, General Vasile Milea.

The General did not belong to Ceausescu's inner circle. The President never fully trusted the army to deal effectively with internal dissent. It was a massive organization, full of unreliable conscripts. Moreover, he had heard rumors for several years about disloyalty within the military high command. Ceausescu had neglected the army in favor of the much smaller and highly trained Securitate force of professionals. The army was poorly trained and equipped while the Securitate had all the latest equipment. Within the Securitate, the dictator had established a crack troop of bodyguards, many of whom had been brought up in orphanages and thought of Elena and Nicolae as their mother and father. The fanatical loyalty of these bodyguards knew no bounds. The Securitate was given precedence over the army regarding internal security.

General Milea, the President's investigators suspected, resented the resources and power bestowed upon the Securitate. They also wondered where the General's ultimate loyalty really lay, with the Ceausescus or the people. The results of the investigation showed that the defense minister was issuing confusing orders to his troops. His commanders were not sure whether or not to shoot.

On the morning of Friday the 22nd, the defense minister attended a high-level meeting at the party headquarters to plan the defense of the capital. The crowds were on their way from University Square. The meeting finished and General Milea made his way to Room 621 on the sixth floor. A secretary handed him top-secret plans for military operations in Bucharest. She left and closed the door. Minutes later a shot rang out. Party officials rushed into the office. The General lay on the floor. Blood pumped from a hole in his chest. An ivory-handled revolver rested near the body. The government issued a communique stating that the General had committed suicide. Many believe he was executed. Ceausescu took comfort. A dangerous traitor had been eliminated. Perhaps now the army would obey the orders of the Commander-in-Chief, Nicolae Ceausescu.

President Ceausescu hoped the death of the unreliable defense minister would end the confusion in the security operations against the demonstrators. But there was now no time to send fresh, unambiguous orders to the troops. While the mortally wounded General lay gasping in Room 621, angry demonstrators surrounded the party headquarters. Party officials panicked and fled in fear of being lynched. Others remained, desperately trying to destroy documents and files. Shouting, firing and burning echoed throughout the building. Revolutionaries entered the building, rushing from room to room, trying to find the leaders. The Securitate chief was found cowering in a third-floor room, guarding himself with a gun. A brave student with an unloaded gun tricked him into surrendering. The intruders looked frantically for Nicolae and Elena. But they were a few steps ahead, on the roof, climbing into a waiting helicopter. Just as the pursuers reached the roof, the gleaming white craft rose into the sky with a bodyguard's pistol pointed at the pilot's head.

The crowds below were overjoyed. The dictator was in flight. The army had refused to fire on the people. Victory celebrations erupted. Romanian flags, minus the Communist symbol in the middle, were hoisted above public buildings. The army and groups of demonstrators took over the TV and radio stations.

While the people of Bucharest were enjoying their first hours of freedom in forty years, a crucial political meeting was taking place behind the scenes. Ion Iliescu, Petre Roman and several other Communist politicians were holding talks with Generals Voinea, Chitac and Militaru. The politicians were all once loyal servants of Ceausescu. But they were now disgruntled, having fallen out of favor with the President. Iliescu had been a powerful secretary of the Communist Party's Central Committee before falling out with Ceausescu, who saw him as a potential rival. In recent years, he had worked as the head of a technical publishing house and was under police surveillance. Though Iliescu had been without political influence for some years, he still had many connections with prominent figures in the Ceausescu regime. He was now making use of them in his negotiations with the generals.

Late in the evening, Iliescu and the generals reached an agreement. At midnight Iliescu announced on Romanian television that a National Salvation Front had been formed and was now in power.

The members of the Second Baptist Church in Oradea, the largest Baptist congregation in Europe, were desperately worried. It was the weekend of December 16, when the revolt first erupted in Timisoara. One of their pastors, Paul Negrut, had gone to Timisoara to lead an evangelistic crusade. His friends and family tried telephoning Timisoara to see how he was. The lines had been cut.

There was nothing on Romanian television about the growing unrest in the country. But the people of Oradea knew, from Hungarian television and Western radio reports, that some kind of trouble had broken out in Timisoara. People started talking of killings. Some members of Paul's church were students at the University in Timisoara. Their parents immediately got into their cars or onto trains to fetch them to safety. Buoyed by the news from Timisoara, demonstrators soon appeared on the streets of Oradea. There was fear, chaos, anger and jubilation.

The Oradea Baptists tried to live as normally as possible in the increasing chaos. They calmly continued going to work, trying to put in a full day as conscientiously as possible. People were astonished. How could anyone take things so calmly when the country was erupting into chaos? The dreaded dictator would soon be back from Iran. He would lead the inevitable crackdown. Some of the army units in Oradea were refusing to shoot demonstrators. The Securitate still shot wildly. People did not dare to believe that they could overthrow the tyrant. He had ruled for a quarter of a century.

Pastor Negrut returned from Timisoara unscathed. While there, he had addressed the anti-government demonstrators, and now he had exciting news for his congregation: "The revolution in Romania began with people on their knees singing Christian songs." When the people of Oradea rose against the regime, Paul was asking to speak to a crowd of 100,000 from a balcony in Oradea's main square. He read the Bible and led them in prayer— 100,000 of them! "There is darkness and sorrow where there is no God," he told the demonstrators. "We came into a time of sorrow through the blood of our parents. Now we are coming out of it through the blood of our children."

In another part of Oradea, Bishop Papp was still making his attacks on Laszlo, right up to the last minute. On Thursday, December 21—the day Ceausescu made his fateful speech in Bucharest—Papp's justificatory statement on Laszlo's eviction was published by the Romanian press agency Agerpres. The bishop denounced him as "an enemy of the Romanian people." Tokes had shown "indiscipline to the higher church forums," he said, "grossly violating the statute of organization and functioning of the Reformed Church in Romania and the laws of the Romanian state." Above all, he accused Laszlo of "denigrating and making a tendentious presentation of the realities in our country."

Papp was still fighting hard to give the regime's version of events to the outside world. He claimed the deportation was justified, as Laszlo had failed to comply with the transferral order or with the judicial ruling for his eviction.

Papp's last verdict was that "it is clear to any person of good faith that Laszlo Tokes broke the oath he took on his ordination. . . . Laszlo Tokes is a victim of his own actions, inspired and encouraged by hostile, anti-Romanian circles abroad, especially Hungary, and under no circumstances can one say that he was sanctioned for his religious activity."

Friday morning's papers carried Bishop Papp's scathing attack.

Peace on Earth?

Monday afternoon, December 18. The Lutheran pastor Hans Dietrich Schullerus of Sura-mica near Sibiu sat down in his office to write his Christmas sermon. His home had no heating. But he did not need to wear a coat. The day was warm. It felt almost like spring. He was gathering his thoughts when his wife—normally very calm—burst into the room. "There has been a big demonstration in Timisoara! There's been shooting!" she cried.

All thoughts of "Peace on Earth" disappeared from Hans's head. Was this true? Just rumors? One heard all kinds of wild stories these days. Hans phoned a friend. He had heard the same. Another hour till the next news broadcast from Radio Free Europe in Munich. The hour dragged on so slowly. Finally it was 7:00 P.M. It was worse

216

than they feared—or was this good news? The beginning of new hope? The dreaded dictator, the self-styled "son of the nation," was abroad visiting the mullahs in Iran. Perhaps he would never return? But Elena, the self-styled "world-renowned and beloved scientist," was still in Bucharest directing the affairs of state.

The next day Pastor Schullerus traveled to the town of Sibiu as usual. Each Tuesday the Lutheran pastors of the district gathered to discuss their sermons. Usually politics was a taboo subject. But this week they could not help talking about events in Timisoara. That evening Pastor Hans and his family listened to Voice of America. For the first time he heard a tape of the uprising in Timisoara. He shuddered as they heard the sounds: the shouts of the angry crowd, the military planes flying low, the whirl of helicopters—and then shooting. First he heard single salvos, then the hacking of automatic weapons. Hans's daughter Susanne put her hands around her head; his wife Anna broke out into tears. His son Volker sat with wide-open eyes and asked, "Why are they doing that?"

On Thursday the 21st, Pastor Hans had business in Sibiu. The children also had an appointment to go to the dentist. On the way, Hans told the children to be careful. The revolution seemed to have passed by Sibiu, where Ceausescu's playboy son Nicu headed the Communist Party. Hans noticed a few animated people talking outside the department store, but he thought nothing of it. He dropped the children off, then went on to the next village, where he had pastoral visits to make. At midday a faithful church member barged in, interrupting the pastor's lunch. There had been shooting in Sibiu, she said.

Hans jumped in his car and headed straight home. Had his children come back home on the bus? he wondered.

The children reached home safely, but they were distressed. Volker was white, Susanne was in tears. They had seen the shooting. The dentist had sent them through the troubled town straight to the bus stop. Hans tried to call his other two children, who were due to return that day via Sibiu. The lines—which never worked well at the best of times—were dead. That night they heard Sibiu mentioned on Western broadcasts for the first time. The revolution had arrived. They were waiting nervously.

Friday morning, December 22. As Hans left his house, he met the mayor and a group of local council officials. They had just left their offices. As he continued on his way, he was brought up suddenly. The sign at the side of the road made him stop and stare. On the slogan "Party, Ceausescu, People," the first two words had been blacked out. Only the People remained. Another sign had been knocked down.

On the way home, Hans heard that the defense minister had shot himself (or had been shot?). A state of emergency had been declared. Every ten minutes Bucharest radio announced proclamations. Hans rushed home and switched on the television. The song "Arise, Romanians. . ." was heard—then a shot of some weary looking people in front of a Romanian flag. A hole was in the middle where the Communist emblem had been cut out. Hans recognized the poet Mircea Dinescu. "Brothers!" the poet declared, "We are in the television building! First we turn to God, who has sent us this wonderful day. The dictator has fled." Cheers filled Hans's house. Moments later portraits of the dictator were being thrown from the windows of the local government offices across the street.

Hans went out onto the street again to see the undreamt-of sight of the dictator's portrait lying on the ground. The frame had come apart and the glass had shattered over the standard, youthful portrait of the ousted dictator. A strange thought came into Hans's head. If only they'd taken the glass out before doing that. He'd been trying to get glass for ages to mend the bedroom window. . . .

On Saturday morning the 23rd, Hans drove to Sibiu to see if his father was all right. On the way he picked up a friend. Her brother was shot the day before in the town. It was a ghostly drive. There was no traffic. Tanks and armored cars sat on the airport runway.

The aviation school was surrounded. Heavily armed soldiers were in view. On the edge of Sibiu, a car flagged him down. Around the Continental Hotel and the theater, a fierce battle was still raging: the Securitate and police against the army. There was no way through. Hans managed to phone his father, who was safe and well, though surrounded by shooting. He could not leave the house and had to stay away from the windows.

Burnt-out cars littered the city center. Saints' pictures hung outside the Catholic church; burning candles and a Christmas tree commemorated the dead. The police and Securitate station was burnt out. Nine years earlier, Hans had spent two days there under interrogation. . . .

It was hard to think of the coming feast. For the first time in forty-two years, Christmas Day was a holiday. "Silent Night, Holy Night" was played on television. Hans remembered the psalm: "Our mouths were filled with laughter, our tongues with songs of joy. . . . The Lord has done great things for us, and we are filled with joy" (Psalm 126:2, 3).

Caught

Friday afternoon, December 22. Nicolae and Elena Ceausescu were on the run. Doubtful about the security at the airport or a military base, Nicolae ordered the helicopter to touch down by a freeway sixty miles from the capital. Brandishing pistols, the Ceausescus and their three bodyguards commandeered a passing car—a red Dacia. Unable to find a loyal Securitate stronghold, they sought help at a house by the side of the road. The minutes seemed like hours as the dispirited fugitives hoped against hope that the Securitate loyalists would reach them before the army.

The army arrived first and the couple was taken to the nearby Boteni military base. "How does it feel, you rats?" shouted one soldier as the captive couple emerged from the military transport vehicle. "Now you will get a taste of your own medicine!" another chipped in.

Nicolae and Elena were unceremoniously dumped in military police cells with ties, belts and shoelaces removed to foil any suicide attempt. What should be done with them? The military command was unsure. For three days the former dictator and his first lady languished there.

Back in Bucharest and in other strongholds of the old regime, celebrations to mark the end of Ceausescu's rule were somewhat premature. Hard-line Securitate agents, who could expect no mercy from the people, struck back with a vengeance. They fought to the death to control

Bucharest and other towns. In the capital, they effectively used underground bunkers and an extensive network of secret tunnels as they mounted guerilla attacks on the army and anti-Ceausescu demonstrators. The Securitate agents could suddenly appear anywhere in the center of Bucharest to commit their bloody deeds. The army led the fight against the better trained and equipped Securitate forces still loyal to Ceausescu. As the days passed, the Securitate appeared to be on the verge of getting the upper hand. Well-armed forces loyal to the Ceausescus were reported to be closing in on their place of detention.

The National Salvation Front government was alarmed. Something had to be done to demoralize the fanatical Ceausescu supporters. The only way to end the bloodshed, the Front concluded, was to sever the head of the Securitate from the body. The Ceausescus must die.

The two-hour show trial was filmed. They sat hunched in their overcoats—the former dictators now knew what ordinary life was like with no indoor heating, even in winter. The couple was tried by a ten-man tribunal, made up mostly of military officers. Nicolae was defiant and unrepentant. He refused to recognize this "court." The sentence was announced. The two were to be executed at once.

Tears streamed down the dictator's face as guards bound his hands behind his back. Elena struggled as her hands were tied. "Don't tie us," she screamed. "My children, you are breaking my hands. It is shameful. Why? Why? I raised you like a mother."

The Grand Conductor and his wife were pushed out of the courtroom into the yard. Elena went first, still struggling, followed by Nicolae. The commander of the firing squad called for four volunteers, but the whole squad stepped forward. As soon as the couple came out of the door, the soldiers lunged forward, opening fire. They even wounded the cameraman. Bullets ripped into Elena's head and body, and she collapsed into a pool of blood. The couple died instantly in the volley of automatic fire. "Cease fire!" the commander shouted from behind. "They've gone mad."

Later in the day, Bucharest radio announced: "The Antichrist is dead! Oh, what wonderful news!" It was Christmas Day.

TWELVE

Liberation

Friday morning, December 22. Edith's parents made the difficult journey from Dej to Mineu in an effort to see their daughter and son-in-law. The Securitate, perhaps sensing the changes in the air, relented and allowed the couple to make a short visit. But while parents and daughter spoke, the Securitate stood behind them, listening to every word. They did not leave them alone together.

Edith's parents had brought sausage and wine for Christmas: Edith and Laszlo could hardly think of the feast ahead. The Securitate watched them closely on Friday morning, so they were unable to find out what was going on by radio.

Interrogations were due to resume that morning. Laszlo expected the worst. He waited nervously for the cars to take them to Zalau. But they didn't show up. Instead, the guards quickly packed up and hightailed it out of Mineu. One of Laszlo's Securitate guards remained behind. He approached Laszlo and said: "Dear sir, if I have wronged you, please don't bear a grudge." Laszlo detected genuine remorse in the agent's voice. They shook hands and the agent disappeared.

It was silent around the house for a few minutes. Laszlo and Edith had no idea what was happening. Then neighbors rushed in. They had seen the television pictures from Bucharest and had seen Ceausescu flee. They knew the old regime was gone. But no one knew just what would replace it. They heard sketchy news about the formation of the transitional government. But it was uncertain just what this would mean.

Soon after the Ceausescus had fled, Bucharest television appealed for anyone with knowledge of Laszlo's whereabouts to call them at once. No one in Bucharest knew where he was. A friend of Laszlo and Edith in Dej, Laci Kerekes, knew. He grabbed the phone. Calling the Dej operator, he immediately asked for a line to the television studio in Bucharest. The operator asked excitedly if he knew where Laszlo was. He said yes.

After twenty anxious minutes of waiting, Laszlo's friend was through to the studio and was able to tell the Romanian people of Laszlo's whereabouts and the details of his interrogation. Laci asked for a bodyguard for Laszlo and Edith. Securitate members were still battling it out in some towns. And some had fled to the hills, where they were continuing guerrilla-style warfare. Laci feared they could mount a revenge attack on Mineu.

In the meantime, the villagers of Mineu all came forward to guard their now world-famous guests. Laszlo and

Edith were exhausted. One long week ago they had been watching the crowds beginning to form outside their window back in Timisoara. They had endured being dragged from their home and church, beatings, deportation, interrogation and threats. Now their captors had fled.

But as Laszlo and Edith tried to rest, the uncertainty was not at an end. The revolution which had started around them had spread and come back to save them. But what would happen now? Ceausescu was still on the run. Would he mount a return bid? Laszlo knew he would be one of the first victims if the old regime regained power. People from nearby villages streamed over to Mineu to join those already guarding Laszlo. They brought axes with them to fight off any counterattack.

Laszlo and Edith gratefully accepted their neighbor's invitation to move in, and this became their home for the next month. The pastor's house had few facilities—the only furniture was what was dumped by the Securitate after the eviction from Timisoara.

On Christmas Eve, the papers published the platform of the National Salvation Front. It promised to establish a multi-party democracy with free elections in the spring. It also pledged itself to guarantee the rights of the national minorities. At the bottom of the platform were listed the names of the new members of the Front's Council. Laszlo was surprised to see his name listed. No one had asked him if he wished to serve. He didn't even know what his responsibilities would be. Some of the former Ceausescu supporters on the council did not impress Laszlo. But the council also included the names of some courageous dissidents such as Doina Cornea and Mircea Dinescu. Laszlo felt it his duty to accept the call and participate in the work of the council. One day Laszlo was Public Enemy Number One, the next he was a member of Romania's governing body.

The Border Opens

The Romanian border guards were baffled. After the outbreak of the revolt in Timisoara that weekend, they had been ordered to seal the borders. On Friday, after the flight of the Ceausescus, they received fresh orders to reopen them. After years of rudeness and hostile searches, the guards suddenly put on a new image of welcome and friendliness. Bare patches marked the walls where Ceausescu's portrait had hastily been removed.

There was a spontaneous movement in Hungary to travel to Transylvania to share the joy of revolution. The roads were lined with cheering people making the "V for victory" sign. The drivers were obliged to return the sign, their arms getting tired with the effort. In Cluj and other cities, people stopped Hungarian cars, handing out leaflets. "No more dictatorship," they read in Romanian. The natives of Cluj apologized that they had none in Hungarian.

Aid started pouring into the country. Much-needed medicines, food and other vital supplies arrived. Some of the first shipments came from Hungarians. The people of Eastern and Western Europe were united in helping the people of Romania. The country that had been isolated for so many years, and whose borders had been sealed for the past week, was now receiving guests. There was a carnival atmosphere. But danger lurked in the mountains. Securitate men on the loose were still attacking foreign cars.

On Saturday, visitors from Hungary arrived in Mineu, along with the first of what were to be many journalists. Laszlo and Edith were tired but pleased to see their visitors. They behaved as though nothing extraordinary had happened to them—perhaps the enormity of the events had not yet sunk in. The journalist, Zoltan Lovas, brought a television crew from Budapest. The weary couple told the camera how they had been dragged here the previous Sunday and how they had had to endure threats and interrogations.

It was cold but crisp outside. Edith stood in front of the pastor's house in the pale winter sun to describe how they had been hauled in by the secret police. To a backdrop of country houses and gardens amid gently rolling hills, Edith spoke calmly and determinedly of everything that had happened. Chickens padded across the grass behind her and farm animals and a sawmill could be heard in the background. A protective guard of villagers surrounded Edith.

She then took the cameraman inside to display the primitive conditions in the house. Their possessions, which had been unceremoniously dumped six days ago, had been tidied up into some order. A few kitchen implements and some tins and jars of food sat on the floor of the empty kitchen. A refrigerator and a broken washing machine were the only modern pieces. Bare whitewashed walls and wooden floorboards showed no luxury. A stack of kitchen plates still sat on the window ledge.

Laszlo then spoke, standing in the shadow of the church. He was dressed in suit and tie but looked disheveled. The experiences of the last few days could be seen on his face: lines of worry marked his forehead. Villagers watched as he addressed the camera. Laszlo wasted no time resuming one of the main themes of his ministry: reconciliation between nationalities. He believed passionately that if the Hungarians and Romanians were to have a future worth living in Transylvania, they must live in peace and harmony. Transylvania was the homeland of both nationalities.

Laszlo spoke to the camera in Romanian: "Those rumors to the effect that we Hungarians of Romania are enemies of the country and are nationalists, chauvinists and irredentists are no more than lies. What happened recently clearly shows that Hungarians joined forces with their Romanian brothers. The most intimate solidarity and spirit of love prevailed between the nationalities. Every Romanian should know that we Hungarians are their friends."

Then the people gathered for an impromptu service in the churchyard. The villagers—mostly men—stood in a circle around Laszlo between the tiny whitewashed church and the wooden belfry built above the gateway to the churchyard. They stood impassively and in silence, clutching their hats in their hands, as Laszlo read from the Scriptures. More and more villagers arrived as they heard Laszlo praying, until more than fifty were there. Edith watched, her hair unwashed, as Laszlo preached.

After the sermon, he led them in the Lord's Prayer. Then he started a hymn, his clear voice leading his new flock. He raised both his hands to bless the people. An old man stepped forward to address Laszlo warmly, clutching him by the hand and not letting him go. Laszlo shook everyone's hand as they left the churchyard.

Laszlo conducted service after service in the days following his liberation. Delegations from nearby villages came to Mineu to hear him preach. Laszlo sent messengers to the clergy of the region inviting all to attend a grand inter-denominational Christmas service in Mineu. Laszlo preached a powerful Christmas sermon of hope fulfilled: "I wait for the Lord. . . . My soul waits for the Lord more than watchmen wait for the morning" (Psalm 130:5, 6), he proclaimed from the pulpit. "This expectation is being fulfilled even now. We believe it and know for certain that we did not wait in vain. The promises are indeed being fulfilled, especially the promise of faith, which is buried in us like a tiny glowing ember beneath the ashes, or like a seed beneath the snow that springs forth and produces its own fruit." Laszlo's eyes had seen the glory of the coming of the Lord. Redeemed by God's grace from his darkest hour, Laszlo had high hopes for the future.

Immediately after the Christmas service he led a delegation to the nearby Orthodox church to express the solidarity of the Hungarian minority with the Romanians. Laszlo returned to this theme when asked for the first time to broadcast a Christmas message on Romanian television. He described the moment when the Romanians joined local Hungarians in Timisoara to defend him before his eviction as "the greatest honor." Romanians and Hungarians had been united by "solidarity, fraternity, our common strength and the oppression that subjugated all of us," he declared.

On the Road

Laszlo was immediately invited to visit other churches in the Mineu area. In January, he went to the village of Volcsok, where he was welcomed for the service by Pastor Sandor Beke. The small village church was filled to overflowing. Both Hungarians and Romanians crammed inside. They were not only from Volcsok but from neighboring villages, too. Soldiers checked the papers of everyone entering the church—armed Securitate fugitives were still at large. Laszlo spoke, followed by Pastor Beke, speaking in both Hungarian and Romanian. Two choirs sang traditional hymns. After the service, the women and children filed out first, then the men, and finally the two pastors.

The crowds streamed into the pastor's house for a special feast. Visitors, too, were invited. The soldiers stayed by Laszlo, even at the table. Laszlo spoke of the need for a renewal of church life.

Laszlo not only visited small villages but also traveled farther afield. Crowds welcomed him to every service he held. Committed to reconciliation between Romanians and Hungarians, he spoke in both languages and was delighted that members of both communities came to hear him.

His old congregation in Dej welcomed him back Thursday, January 11, 1990. It was the first service he had taken in the church since being dismissed by Bishop Nagy in 1984. About 2,000 people squeezed into the church, with another 5,000 standing in the cold outside. Two soldiers followed Laszlo into the church, their guns at the ready. As he sat below the pulpit on the minister's bench, the two sat on either side of him, removing their caps. As Laszlo ascended the steps to speak, the two moved forward to stand below the pulpit.

Laszlo chose the same text he had used on the occasion of his first service in Dej back in 1977. He preached from 1 Kings 19: the story of Elijah being comforted by an angel in the desert after fleeing from Jezebel. After the service, Laszlo spoke for five minutes—in Hungarian and Romanian—about everything that had happened to him. Later, the members of the church council, his friends from the youth group and others crowded into the pastor's house nearby. There was earnest talk of the future of their church, as well as lighthearted reminiscing.

In early January, some members of the Timisoara church traveled up to Mineu to see Laszlo. The joy of their meeting was great—until then Laszlo did not know who was alive and who was dead. Now he was able to find out what had happened after he had been so unceremoniously dragged away in the early hours of the morning of December 17. Laszlo was sorry to hear that the mood of Timisoara was subdued. The euphoria of revolution had given way to sadness at the deaths of more than a hundred people in the sudden violence.

Makeshift shrines commemorated the places where the victims had fallen. Relatives had hung portraits of the dead on lampposts and decorated them with flowers and ribbons. Crude wooden crosses were carved with the dates of birth and death of the victims—always December 1989. Laszlo was also sad to learn his congregation had been unable to celebrate Christmas properly without a pastor.

Laszlo was eager to return to his beloved congregation in Timisoara. But the security situation, still uncertain, meant a round-the-clock armed guard. This was strange for Laszlo—he was used to being watched and followed by the security organs, not being protected. He had to wait for word from Timisoara that it was safe to return.

From early January, Laszlo received death threats. He assumed they were from embittered Ceausescu loyalists. Soon after Christmas, he traveled to Bucharest for the first session of the full Council of the National Salvation Front. On the way home the train carriage he should have been in was shot at. The rest of the train was untouched.

It was not until January 28 that Laszlo was back in his Timisoara church for the usual Sunday service. The church was packed, and the local radio station provided loudspeakers for the crowds outside on the street. A church delegation from Hungary was present, as were faithful worshipers from surrounding villages. Aaron Ady, an old man in his seventies, traveled the long road from Mineu to be there. He wanted to get to know Laszlo's community in Timisoara.

International Statesman

On February 2, Laszlo set out on his first trip abroad since the age of 14. The people of Hungary gave him a hero's welcome. For eleven days he traveled to numerous towns under the strictest security measures. In the city of Debrecen, known by the Hungarians as the Calvinist Rome, Laszlo was received with honor. The Debrecen Reformed Academy awarded him an honorary doctorate in recognition of his activity. More than 25,000 people gathered to hear Laszlo preach. In Budapest, politicians, churchmen, journalists, writers and intellectuals all went out of their way to meet him.

But events in Romania were never far away during his triumphant visit to Hungary. He had to take a day out to rush back to Bucharest to meet the visiting United States Secretary of State, James Baker, who was holding talks in Romania. Laszlo was assuming the role of an international statesman.

The trip to Hungary was the start of a series of foreign tours that would take him to Czechoslovakia, Belgium, Holland, France, and North America.

Laszlo was overwhelmed by his reception in the United States and Canada in March and April. He had been hoping to take some time out to relax with his brother Stephen. They had many missing years to catch up on. But the tight schedule allowed him little time to put his feet up. Interviews, meetings, lectures, sermons, dinners, awards—all were crammed into his three-week whistle-stop tour. The highlight of the visit was the meeting in the White House with President George Bush and Secretary of State James Baker. In Canada he held talks with Prime Minister Brian Mulroney.

On the way back from his North American tour, the exhausted Laszlo stopped off in Geneva for meetings at the World Council of Churches. It was a bittersweet stop for Laszlo. He was now the honored guest of an institution that used to bestow honor on the old, discredited leaders of his Church. The World Council was then discussing the effects of the changes in Eastern Europe on the churches. Laszlo did not mince his words. He repeated his attacks on Western church bodies for failing to speak up about abuses under the Ceausescu regime. He attacked the organization for compromising with the Ceausescu regime. Communists in Eastern Europe had been working for "the death of the Christian faith," he told them. He warned against church leaders in Romania who had compromised with Ceausescu and yet remained in office.

Laszlo was particularly disappointed in the World Alliance of Reformed Churches, which is closely allied to

the World Council of Churches. "One of the biggest dis-
appointments of my life," he declared, "has been to experience the total lack of support from official church bodies
abroad. Neither the World Council of Churches nor the
World Alliance of Reformed Churches was willing to support me. . . . Any protest to Ceausescu would have been of
help. But in Geneva they were not interested in this single pastor's fight for freedom. To them I was an unknown
village pastor . . . a disturbing element who had been
quarreling with his bishops for years."

And he went on to describe a disturbing parallel: "I
remember well the assistance we contributed in the
struggle against apartheid in South Africa. My Church
stood by the black freedom fighters. Allan Boesak, the
President of the World Alliance of Reformed Churches,
gave us credit for this. However, when the struggle was
raging for life or death in Romania, he and the other
ecumenical heavyweights let us down."

The Geneva headquarters of the Reformed Alliance,
Laszlo said, knew that the leadership of the Reformed
Church in Romania was corrupt. However, they had re-
ceived Bishop Papp in the West as an honored guest.

Laszlo's disappointment had been shared by many
Eastern European Christian dissidents over the years.
International church bodies were quick to condemn human rights violations in right-wing dictatorships. But
they showed poor judgment in turning a blind eye to
abuses in Communist countries. The delegates from Communist countries—all of them there with government
approval—almost always blocked any attempt to discuss
religious rights in their lands.

The revolution might have come about sooner, Laszlo
believed, if pressure had been exerted in the West. "This

is my accusation against the churches of the West—our revolution did not come about with their help but in spite of their unwillingness to fight for the truth." He called—without arrogance—for international church bodies to repent and ask for forgiveness.

Laszlo arrived back in Romania, exhausted but exhilarated, on April 1, just in time to celebrate his thirty-eighth birthday.

Vision for the Church

The churches of Romania have a critically important role in Laszlo's vision for the future. For many years he had dreamed of renewed churches igniting the renewal of society. Even to Laszlo, this sometimes seemed to be just a pipe dream. But now the signs were promising. The tiny ember beneath the ash appeared to glow hotter and brighter.

The Romanian revolution brought about not only the downfall of Ceausescu but of his servants in the Reformed Church as well. Bishop Papp vanished; no one knew where to. When demonstrators broke into his house in Oradea on December 22, they found the bishop and his wife gone. The young people found only his aged mother-in-law, sitting crying at the table. They told her they would not harm her. She was sent to some relatives and died soon afterward. Demonstrators daubed slogans on the outside of his house: "Traitor" and "Murderer."

Bishop Nagy, less embarrassed than Papp about his past, had merely resigned his office. By these actions the two had confirmed their close links—if there was still any doubt—with the old regime.

The departure of the two Reformed bishops, Papp and Nagy, was welcomed by many. This now left the urgent task of renewing the leadership. Laszlo was immediately spoken of as a possible candidate, despite his youth. His views on the need for a reconstitution of the leadership were well-known. His non-compromising stand against the old regime was beyond doubt.

But there were obstacles. As a general synod of the Church gathered in Cluj on January 30, 1990, there were some who tried to obstruct the proceedings. While Laszlo was immensely popular among the faithful at the grass roots, the old Church bureaucracy was somewhat fearful of him. Many of the clergy were also rather jealous. Laszlo was duly elected Bishop of Oradea on March 29 in the first constitutional episcopal election for decades. The Dean of Tirgu Mures, Kalman Csiha, was elected to succeed Gyula Nagy as Bishop of Cluj.

In a move that signaled a desire for an end to autocratic rule by the bishops, the general synod of the Reformed Church decided to reduce the term of a bishop to four years and to limit the number of terms to two.

It was only in March, 1990, that Papp resurfaced—he was staying with one of his sons near the French city of Metz. Describing Laszlo as a "megalomaniac" and an "awkward customer," he upheld his actions.

He justified his closeness to the Ceausescu regime by quoting from Paul's letter to the Romans: "Everyone must submit himself to the governing authorities, for there is no authority except that which God has established. The authorities that exist have been established by God" (Romans 13:1). Those resisting state authority, Papp maintained, cannot justify it by religious faith.

Bishop Nagy, meanwhile, lived a quiet life in Cluj, still maintaining that he had not done anything wrong.

The Romanian Orthodox Church had been even more extensively infiltrated by the Communists than the Reformed Church. Despite the avowed atheism of the regime, the privileged status of the Orthodox Church made it almost the state church. Ceausescu brought in a bishop and thirteen priests for the televised funeral of his father in 1982. This was a role the Orthodox Church had always played in the brief history of the modern Romanian state—before the Communists it had been vocal in its support for the right-wing regime which had preceded it. Orthodox bishops were renowned for their sycophantic public praise of Ceausescu and his policies. Even at the grass-roots level, Orthodox priests often cooperated with the Securitate against the small evangelical churches and the banned Uniate Church.

After the December revolution, the role of the Orthodox Patriarch Teoctist came under strong attack. He had ruled the Church since 1986 and was now being accused of being a pillar of support for Ceausescu's rule. The new Minister of Culture, Andrei Plesu, publicly invited him to retire to a monastery. Romanian students, joined the criticism of Teoctist and of other members of the hierarchy.

Under Teoctist's leadership, the Church had issued frequent telegrams of praise to Ceausescu that bordered on the blasphemous. The president was described in almost divine terms. The government's policies were loudly praised. Systematization, the bishops said, assured the modernization of people's lives while preserving the glorious past that is part of the country's national heritage.

Teoctist was in the forefront of the government's campaign to convince the world that there was complete religious freedom in Romania and that Romanian citizens enjoyed full human rights. Speaking at an interdenominational conference in Bucharest on August 1, 1989, he had "emphasized the religious freedom which the religions in Romania have enjoyed during the last forty-five years, in which they could unfold their activity unhampered."

The painful reassessment of the Church's role in the Ceausescu era had begun. The process was to prove bitter and divisive. "It is all false," Teoctist responded to charges of collaboration. "I simply defended the Church against Communism."

Teoctist declared that his Church had also been a victim of the old regime, suffering greatly. "The slightest disobedience on the part of priests or monks was punished with long and frequent detentions." He said he had been trying for three years to meet Ceausescu but had constantly been told he was too busy. He went on to claim that, after the massacre of civilians in December during the revolution, he had been on the verge of sending a telegram to Ceausescu calling on him to halt the killing. But then he heard the dictator had already fled.

"In the past twenty-five years," he admitted, "we have lived through shocking moments, and I did not have the courage the youth have shown."

The feelings of guilt were echoed by other church leaders such as Bishop Albert Klein of the German Lutheran Church in Romania. On December 22, he declared on behalf of the Church leadership: "We are concerned about our own guilt."

How far had church leaders sought to protect their people, and when did that turn into collaboration? One pastor explained, "We were all forced to make compromises. But some, instead of making one step, made two or more—out of fear, career reasons or why ever not?" Another pastor, Zsolt Raduch of the Hungarian Lutherans, put it like this: "During the totalitarian regime, we wanted no dead heroes. We wanted to preserve Church members for the future."

The small Jewish community also raised questions about the veteran Chief Rabbi Moses Rosen, who had headed the community for the past forty-one years. The seventy-seven-year-old Rosen strongly denied any allegations that he had behaved at all improperly during the Ceausescu era. He declared that he had to hide his dislike of Ceausescu and somehow work with the regime: "The life of my people was in his hands." Despite his propaganda role on behalf of the regime, he was credited with preserving Jewish life and institutions.

It was mainly abroad that the disputes over Rosen's role took place. One irony of his life's work was that most of his flock—400,000—had been given permission to emigrate to Israel. By the time of the revolution in December, 1989, the pre-war community of 800,000 had been reduced to fewer than 20,000.

The Eastern-rite Catholic Church had refused to compromise with the regime—and it had been banned as far back as 1948. Its bishops and priests had endured years of imprisonment and banishment as a result of their loyalty to the Pope and their Church. Their example became a powerful witness to members of other churches.

One of the first acts of the new regime in the sphere of

religion was to revoke the decree of December 1, 1948, that banned the Catholic Church. The Church's secret bishops gradually reemerged from hiding to lead their revived Church. The 2 million faithful could again worship in public—although only in the open air, since they had no church buildings.

Another of the first acts was to make Christmas Day a public holiday—for the first time in forty-two years. This brought instant hope to Romania's hard-pressed Christians. Under Ceausescu, Christmas Day had been a regular working day. The cheerless "Winter Tree Festival" was nothing to look forward to. Carols echoed from the television and radio for the first time in decades.

Christians were soon making up for the lost years. Pastors and priests had been in the thick of the revolution. They had joined revolutionaries on the balconies of prominent buildings in many towns and cities across the country, leading the people in prayer. Churches began evangelistic crusades. Christians abroad packed Bibles and Christian books in their truckloads of aid. Congregations that had been denied permission to build new churches immediately started drawing up plans. New church papers were planned.

Back in Timisoara, Laszlo's life was an endless round of activity. He had the parish to care for, as well as streams of visitors, journalists, bearers of aid. Two soldiers stood guard at the doors of the church office. A third with a submachine gun stood inside at the door of the apartment.

THIRTEEN

The New Romania

The near universal jubilation at the overthrow of Ceausescu began to dissipate as Ion Iliescu and the National Salvation Front consolidated its grip on power in the winter of 1989/1990. After the initial post-revolution euphoria began to subside, Laszlo realized that Romania's road to democracy would be rockier than it was for East Germany, Czechoslovakia and Hungary. It was not just that the leadership of the National Salvation Front was made up of ex-Communists. But its behavior revealed deeply ingrained authoritarian instincts.

Laszlo had no serious qualms about many of the first policy decisions of the new government. Its decision to execute the Ceausescus, its redistribution of badly needed food to hungry consumers in Romania rather than foreign markets, its banning of the Communist Party and its abolition of the death sentence were all genuinely welcomed. But Laszlo noticed certain omissions. The Ili- escu regime was reluctant to replace Communists who were known to have abused their power during the Ceausescu era with capable and respected men and women. The Front was also reluctant to honor its com- mitment to guarantee the rights of the minority nation- alities. Moreover, Laszlo observed that the leadership of the Front was inclined to use the methods of the Com- munists to achieve its ends. The secret police still seemed to be in business, listening in to telephone calls, inter- cepting mail and gathering information.

The Front's Council, which Laszlo agreed to partici- pate in, lacked any real power. Dominated by former Communists and their fellow travelers, the council was little more than a debating society that in the end rubber- stamped the policies of Iliescu and his government. Front officials continued to govern by decree, often without con- sulting the full council. This was how Ceausescu and his fascist predecessors had governed.

Laszlo was alarmed by the decision of the Front to turn itself into a political party and stand for election in the spring. He and all the people of Romania had been led to believe by Iliescu that the Front was no more than a transitional coalition, the function of which was to main- tain stability in the country until free elections produced a new government. Now it seemed the ex-Communist leaders of the Front were intent on retaining power for themselves and other members of the old Communist es- tablishment.

Signs that the revolution did not mean a complete break with the past also appeared in church life. Instead of abolishing the hated Department of Religious Affairs, the Iliescu regime upgraded it into a government ministry. Instead of diminishing the number of its officials, the new Ministry employed more people than the old Department. The Ministry retained power to interfere in church life, to grant or refuse state recognition to denominations and religious associations.

The Ministry granted legal recognition to the newly formed Evangelical Alliance of Romania only after a long drawn-out campaign, which resulted in embarrassment for the regime abroad. While the government "unbanned" the Eastern-rite Catholic Church, it dragged its feet on granting full legal recognition and returning its confiscated church property. The newly appointed head of the Ministry, Nicolae Stoicescu, set out to restore the strong alliance between the Orthodox Church, of which he was a strident member, and the Romanian state. Patriarch Teoctist reemerged from his premature retirement to resume his leadership of the Orthodox Church. Teoctist and Stoicescu both desired an Orthodox-state alliance to keep at bay the growing influence of the evangelical churches and the Eastern-rite Catholic Church. The privileged position of the Orthodox Church was endangered by the growth of these two rival religious forces.

Many prominent people who were willing to support the Front in the immediate aftermath of the revolution were now dissociating themselves from it. The heroic Romanian dissident from Cluj, Doina Cornea, quit the Front's Council in disgust. She found that the Front's tightly controlled radio and television stations would not report alternative views. The revolution had not swept censorship out of Romania. Doina was a genuine democrat and would have none of this. Baptist pastor Paul

Negrut of Oradea quit the local Council of the National Salvation Front. He was particularly alarmed by the Front's publicly stated commitment to promote humanism. Was this just another word for atheism? he wondered. In Negrut's scheme of things, God comes before man. He could not advocate humanism.

Tough Decision

Laszlo had a dilemma. On the one hand, he was willing to cooperate, at least temporarily, with all members of society, including ex-Communists, to ensure that the unstable country did not drift into bloody chaos. Surely, reconciliation is what the country now needs, he thought. But how could he continue to support a governing body that paid mere lip service to cooperation while establishing a virtual monopoly of power for itself? Laszlo began to criticize the Front. In mid-January he charged in a radio interview that the Front was not adequately defending the rights of minorities. He warned that it would be making a grave mistake if it were to continue acting as if other political parties and interest groups did not exist. Laszlo, too, turned his back on the Front.

Meanwhile, relations between Hungarians and Romanians were rapidly deteriorating. Many Romanians throughout the country were prepared to give Laszlo and the Reformed congregation in Timisoara credit for their crucial role in the overthrow of Ceausescu. But once the Hungarians began to make concrete proposals for the restoration of minority rights, many Romanians began to feel threatened. Decisions made at the local level to restore Hungarian as the language of instruction in previously Romanianized schools and to import textbooks—especially history books—were widely resented within the Romanian community. Non-Hungarian-speaking students and teachers would have to leave these schools. "Do the Hungarians now want to take over?" "They ought to remember this is Romania, not Hungary!" These were the thoughts of many Romanians. Even the enlightened Doina Cornea fell out with Laszlo over the issue of the reestablishment of a Hungarian language university in Cluj.

Radical Romanian nationalist organizations sprang up. They demanded that only Romanian should be used as an official language in public life and opposed state support for Hungarian national institutions and organizations. The Romanian nationalist group Vatra Romaneasca began holding public rallies that had strong anti-Hungarian overtones. "One country, one language!" "We are people, Hungarians are rubbish!" Such cries could be heard on the streets at the close of Vatra rallies.

Hungarians began to feel threatened in areas like Cluj, Tirgu Mures and Satu Mare, where Vatra's influence was strong. "During the Ceausescu era we lived in fear of terror from above. Now we live in terror from our own neighbors," bewailed a young Hungarian resident of Cluj. Perhaps the death threats were not just threats of ex-Securitate fugitives, Laszlo wondered. Maybe they represented widespread feelings among the Romanian population.

The seething nationality conflict exploded in Tirgu Mures in mid-March. March 15 is the Hungarian national day, commemorating the beginning of the Hungarian Revolution of 1848. The Hungarians of Transylvania were eager to celebrate their national day freely for the first time in over four decades. For Vatra Romaneasca members, this was a provocation. They were particularly offended because during the Revolution of 1848 the Hungarian nation demanded the union of Transylvania with Hungary. Vatra radicals warned the Hungarians not to make too much of their celebrations in public.

In some towns the Hungarians canceled their celebrations or scaled them down. But in Tirgu Mures they went ahead as planned. Moreover, many young people from Hungary arrived, insensitively shouting calls for the return of Transylvania to Hungary. Barbaric violence cut short the celebrations. Vatra thugs mercilessly attacked Hungarians. Shouts of "Hungarians out of here!" and "Death to Tokes" could be heard throughout the town. Dozens were killed. Romanian mobs broke into the offices of the Democratic Federation of Hungarians of Romania and created mayhem. The well-known Hungarian poet Andras Suto suffered a serious eye injury from his beating. The violence and bloodshed continued for days. The pall of a pogrom hung over the town.

Why didn't the authorities act energetically to restore order? Did the government secretly sympathize with the anti-Hungarian thugs, or was it just fearful of losing popularity among the Romanian majority? Laszlo and most Hungarians in Transylvania lost what little faith they had left in the National Salvation Front.

The Hungarians were not the only people to express their dissatisfaction with the new regime. Thousands of students and others protested against the new leaders in the capital. They, too, paid dearly for their defiance. A group of protesters had begun their sit-in in central Bu-

charest on April 22. They remained there, defiantly ignoring slanders against them (put out by Romanian
television) that they were fascists and good-for-nothings
who were engaged in theft, black marketeering and open
sex. Iliescu's description of them as "hooligans" infuri-
ated them. But it was his decision to clear them by force
that showed the world his gut reactions. When soldiers
failed to dislodge them a few days before his inauguration as president, Iliescu arranged for large numbers of
club-wielding miners to be brought into the capital to end
the protests.

As the TV cameras of the world rolled, out-of-control
miners laid into everyone they could find with batons and
sticks. The indiscriminate brutality was effective: the
demonstrators were removed. They fled or were taken to
hospitals with serious injuries. At least five people—the
new government was not honest with the figures—were
killed. The headquarters of the Peasants' Party and the
Liberals were wrecked. So were the offices of opposition
newspapers, including the independent *Romania Libera.*
Iliescu thanked the miners. The prime minister, Petre
Roman, put on a more subdued face for the international
media, regretting the violence. The United States and
the European Community signaled their unease. In protest, the U.S. ambassador boycotted President Iliescu's
inauguration June 20.

The Democratic Federation

Just a few weeks before the riots in Tirgu Mures,
Laszlo had been elected Honorary President of the Democratic Federation of Hungarians of Romania. The Feder-

ation was founded soon after the downfall of Ceausescu. It aimed to promote Hungarian representation in government, the use of Hungarian in schools, the media, and public administration. At its first meeting, the Federation declared that "the Hungarians in Romania wish to form their future solidarity with the Romanian people on the basis of mutual respect and understanding."

The Federation originally did not foresee itself as a political party. But once the National Salvation Front began to show its true colors, the Federation decided to participate fully in political life. Laszlo hoped that as time passed there would be no need for him to play a prominent role in politics. He did not wish to become a professional politician. He knew that first and foremost his role must be as a minister of God. However, he believed that the situation in Romania was so critical that withdrawal from political life was not a real option. There was no contradiction between belief and politics, he reasoned. He saw that politics affected every aspect of life. If complete disengagement was impossible, he thought, then courageous participation was the only way forward.

After the bloody Tirgu Mures events, Laszlo became convinced that Romania was on the road to civil war if the National Salvation Front did not steer away from dictatorial rule. He believed that the revolution begun in December had stopped unfinished. Romania, he thought, needed a second revolution, but it had to be peaceful. Existing political institutions had to be used.

Laszlo tinkered with the idea of running for president in the spring elections. He knew that, as a Hungarian, he had no chance of winning. This was more true than ever now that ethnic Romanians were turning away from him in droves. But perhaps his candidacy would give him a national platform and have some symbolic value. This idea was scuttled by Laszlo and his supporters in the Democratic Federation of Hungarians of Romania.

Laszlo ran instead for the Senate as a candidate of the Federation. He refused to run in a district where there was a Hungarian majority and election almost guaranteed. He chose to run in Timisoara. It was there his revolution began, and it was from there he wished to see it through to completion. Although the Hungarians were not as numerous in the Timisoara district as in some parts of Transylvania, he had high hopes of victory. Anti-Hungarian sentiment was fairly low there. The National Salvation Front was unpopular among all the nationalities of the area. Laszlo was still regarded affectionately as a local hero by many Romanians who knew Laszlo as a tireless worker for good community relations.

The May 20 elections revealed that Romania had a long way to go before it could count itself as a member of the community of democratic European nations. Violence, intimidation and fraud were the order of the day, most of it committed on behalf of the National Salvation Front. Prominent and popular opposition candidates— both Hungarian and Romanian—such as Laszlo's good friend and lawyer Elod Kincses were disqualified from standing for election on technical grounds. When the results of the voting came in, Laszlo was bitterly disappointed. He had failed in his bid to be elected to the Senate. He lost by 11,000 votes. A total of 53,000 votes had been suspiciously invalidated by the authorities. Laszlo was shattered by the defeat. He had thought that more Romanians shared his ideals of democracy and reconciliation. The Germans of the Timisoara district showed little interest in the election. Many did not even vote at all. They were waiting for emigration papers for West Germany.

Even more depressing for Laszlo was the result of the national election. The National Salvation Front scored a landslide victory with over 66 percent of the vote. Laszlo's Democratic Federation of Hungarians of Romania came in second, but with a mere 7 percent. What worried Laszlo most was not the countless electoral irregularities. While these contributed to the scale of the Front's overwhelming victory at the polls, they were not entirely responsible. The fact was that more Romanians voted for the Front of their own free will. Principles of democracy had yet to penetrate the surface of the political consciousness of the population.

The New Bishop

Two weeks before the disastrous election, Laszlo savored a moment of glory—one that surpassed any possible political triumph. On May 8, 1990, Laszlo was installed as Bishop of Oradea, the successor to his persecutor, Laszlo Papp. It was a proud day for all those who had supported Laszlo and longed for the renewal of the Reformed Church under new leadership. Laszlo's new church in Oradea was packed to overflowing for the installation service. Entry to the church was by ticket only. Laszlo's family was there, as were many people from his Timisoara congregation. Clergymen from other churches as well as delegations from abroad squeezed into the full church. A direct link to a culture club next door brought the service live to an overflow congregation. Still this was not enough as crowds thronged the street outside— young people, simple people from villages miles away.

Beginning his inaugural sermon, Laszlo quoted God's tender words from Scripture: "I have redeemed you; I have summoned you by name; you are mine" (Isaiah 43:1). He offered his thanks to God and thanked the congregations that had elected him as bishop. He remembered his grandparents and parents, publicly acknowledging that it was in his family that he learned to serve his Church and his people. His parents gave him a model of humanity and courage.

He gave as his motto, "With God for the people." This, he said, was the guiding force for himself and his wife. Just as it had led them during the revolution in Timisoara, so it would lead them in the future.

Laszlo looked forward under the new regime to a religious rebirth after one of the darkest periods of their history. He likened his Timisoara congregation to David and his defeat of Goliath. Now, he said, the living Word of God was needed to pour faith and hope into those who are discouraged. "A mighty fortress is our God," Laszlo declared in the words of Martin Luther. He told the thousands gathered for the service that a firm foundation was needed to build the Church of the future.

Years of fighting against the superior power of the dictatorship had taken its toll on the Church, Laszlo said. Some people died fighting; others were weak or ran away. Church institutions disintegrated. The youth slipped away. Anxiety and fear gripped Church members. The first step on the way toward revival of the Church was repentance. Laszlo called for a community-wide repentance.

The Church needed to think as a whole. In some parts of Transylvania it had more or less died out. Laszlo highlighted the need for a census to find out the exact situation of the Church and its members. He recognized that the Church had become too clerical. Too much power had been concentrated in the hierarchy and there was an urgent need to democratize and decentralize the Church. Each congregation needed to be completely autonomous.

In an obvious reference to the abuses of Papp and Nagy in the recent past, he called for limitations on the bishop's power. The presidency of the synod and church disciplinary matters should be taken out of the hands of the bishop. He supported the need for a new constitution that would incorporate the changes.

In contrast to the past, when leaders of various churches came together only at meetings of support for Ceausescu, Laszlo proposed developing free interdenominational links with other churches within Transylvania. He also pledged to draw closer to other Reformed churches among the Hungarian minorities in Czechoslovakia, Yugoslavia and the Carpathian region of the Ukraine.

Real freedom of religion would come only with the complete autonomy of the church. The aim, he told the congregation in the Oradea church, was "a free church in a free state." Financial and political dependence on the state had done great damage to the church.

Laszlo called for the Church to return to the sphere of religious education of the young and social service. New church buildings were needed, especially in new districts of towns. Over the past fifty years, many villagers had moved to the towns, and whole districts had been built where the Communists did not allow one new church to be built. New church publications were also needed to educate and inform the people.

Laszlo also referred to a matter which concerned himself as well as others. On December 28 a group of Church members had issued a call that all those who had been unjustly disciplined by the Church under pressure from the state should be rehabilitated by the Church's disciplinary bodies. It was ironic that Laszlo should be standing here in the pulpit of the Oradea church as bishop to repeat this call.

Laszlo finished his address with the words of the prophet Nehemiah to those building a wall to defend Jerusalem: "The work is extensive and spread out, and we are widely separated from each other along the wall. Wherever you hear the sound of the trumpet, join us there. Our God will fight for us!" (Nehemiah 4:19, 20).

People cried as they witnessed this great event in the life of their Church. Hungarian television was there to record it. Afterward, interviewers talked to people in the street. One of them spoke to a local Romanian, who said: "It's no big deal. Go back home!"

Speaking to journalists after the inauguration, Laszlo likened the Communist era to the Babylonian captivity for the Church. Now the situation was like the wandering in the desert—the people had yet to reach the Promised Land. Laszlo repeated his belief that the tyranny was well behind them but there was a lot to do yet before Romania reached a fully democratic future.

The role of the Church, Laszlo told journalists, was to

fulfill a prophetic role—to take the role of Moses. The Church was the only institution that survived Communism. It should now assume its historical role, as it did in Poland or East Germany.

Laszlo's new style of management was immediately apparent in the bishop's office. He and his new deputy bishop, Attila Veres-Kovacs, adopted a more relaxed and open style of leadership. The stately offices where Papp had barricaded himself against the members of his Church were now accessible to all. Most of the staff was new, including the typists and bookkeepers. The pastors around Papp all resigned their office jobs.

In Papp's day, no one was allowed to enter his office. Laszlo left it as it was when Papp hurriedly departed. He did not change the heavy furniture, the leather armchairs with the stuffing coming out of the seats, the huge, glass-topped desk with the heavy black telephone. And Laszlo immediately asked the authorities for the return of the original bishop's residence, taken away by the Communists in 1962. It was there that he planned on making his new office. He wrote first to the mayor of Oradea, who replied that only the Minister of Religious Affairs could decide the question of its return. The reply came back from Bucharest that Laszlo should be patient—the matter would be resolved.

Laszlo met once a week with his new staff to discuss how they should run the Church—all were new to the job and even Laszlo was learning. Unlike Papp, he sought and listened to the advice of his colleagues. Some of the older pastors in the district found it hard at first to get used to the new, younger leadership. It was difficult to defer to men half their age.

But, after years of neglect and demoralization, the Reformed Church had a new leadership capable of tackling the decline. Laszlo and his colleagues understood the problems. As an old, historic church—and a persecuted one—it had suffered from its failure to renew itself. It had become cut off from the people, partly through the population drift from the villages to the towns, partly through its own lack of enthusiasm and sense of mission. Above all, it had lost the young people who were so vital to its future. A whole generation had grown up without the church. The state had been largely successful in its plot to keep the younger generation apart from the church.

Already a sudden rush for entry to the now-unrestricted seminary had begun. Some of those who were refused admission earlier by the Securitate could now enter, but most of the new students represented fresh blood. But it would take years to bring back the youth to the Church at the grass-roots level. Laszlo's ability with youth and experience would equip him for the task of inspiring the young.

The restrictions on the church have largely been lifted and it has been able to emerge from its enforced isolation. The conditions now exist for renewal.

FOURTEEN

Whys and Wherefores

Of all of 1989's revolutions in Eastern Europe, Romania's was the most violent, most unexpected and—to many—the most disappointing. Why should this be so? The Romanian revolution, and Laszlo Tokes's part in it, has raised many questions.

Ceausescu's rule began on a hopeful note in 1965. The mass murders and arrests of the Stalinist era had begun to recede into the past. For a moment the air seemed easier to breathe. The dismally low living standards rose somewhat. More food and "luxury" items, such as coffee and cigarettes, appeared in the shabby state-run shops. Ceausescu's refusal to send Romanian troops to participate in the Warsaw Pact's 1968 invasion of Czechoslovakia prompted some to think here was a man prepared to break the mold of the past.

Setting the Stage for Revolution

By the end of the 1970s, the bubble had burst. The relative prosperity of the late sixties and seventies had given way to economic depression. The modest consumer goods that had raised the spirits of the population had been subsidized by large foreign loans. The loans had to be repaid. Ceausescu did so with a vengeance. Rapid repayment became a maniacal obsession of the dictator. Romania's increasingly rusty socialist economy could not pay off the debt by increased productivity. High debt repayments plus low productivity equaled grinding poverty for the people of Romania in the 1980s.

With the illusion of a socialist economic miracle shattered, Ceausescu had a few other means to keep the population under control. He invested heavily in promoting Marxist-Leninist ideology. His aim was to create the "new socialist man." This policy failed even more miserably than his economic policies. Many paid lip service to the Marxist creed, but few were genuinely converted. Ceausescu used the cult of personality to greater effect. Everywhere the people turned there was the Grand Conducator: on television, in the newspapers, in books, on posters, in museums. Nicolae and Elena took on the airs and trappings of an emperor and empress. At times they were addressed almost as a god and goddess by their court of admirers. In a land where superstition abounds, many of the simple folk were in awe of the Ceausescus' terrible image. But Ceausescu's most important pillar of support was the security apparatus. The use of violence

258

was widespread and indiscriminate. Sometimes it was physical violence. At other times it was psychological and emotional intimidation. The whole population was touched in one way or another. Sustained, organized political opposition became virtually impossible.

But the cunning power politics of Ceausescu do not explain everything. To suggest otherwise would give Ceausescu more credit than he deserves. Centuries of oppressive foreign domination combined with the spirit of Orthodox fatalism have produced a Romanian culture without a strong revolutionary tradition. Through the ages, the Romanian people have been inclined to accept their lot. From time to time the patience of the common man has snapped under the weight of intolerable oppression, unleashing a sudden and frenzied torrent of violence against the authorities. But such uprisings, like the peasant uprising of Gyorgy Dozsa in the sixteenth century, failed to materialize into successful revolutions. Unlike the English, American and French revolutionaries of the past, the Romanian rebels had no coherent program for the future or durable institutions upon which a new society could be built.

The Hungarians of Transylvania have a stronger revolutionary tradition than their Romanian neighbors. Many struggles were fought by Hungarian princes of Transylvania against Habsburg monarchs in defense of the Hungarian constitution. Protestantism gave spiritual and intellectual backing to Hungarian revolutionary tendencies. It was no accident, then, that the Romanian revolution started outside a Protestant Church in Transylvania and only spread later to the capital, Bucharest.

Laszlo's Role

What kind of credit can Laszlo Tokes take for the over-throw of the Ceausescu regime? He was not the only courageous dissident in Romania. The college professor Doina Cornea and the poet Mircea Dinescu—both ethnic Romanians—resolutely defied the Ceausescu regime. But Laszlo had something they did not have: a power base at the grass-roots level. Laszlo's power base was his congregation. The Reformed Church folk of Timisoara were ready to defend their pastor at great risk to themselves. Why were they willing to do so? Laszlo was a dynamic pastor whose fearless preaching of the Truth inspired the confidence and devotion of his growing flock. But the congregation was defending more than just the person of its popular pastor. By standing up for Laszlo, the faithful were defending the historic rights of Reformed congregations against the encroachments of bishops and the rights of the Reformed Church against state interference.

After the broadcast of Laszlo's "Panorama" interview his power base expanded. From then on Laszlo became a hero of the entire Hungarian nationality, both in Hungary and in Transylvania. Whereas most other dissidents in Romania were largely isolated and had little active support outside intellectual circles, Laszlo Tokes became a household name among Hungarians as a symbol of national resistance to Romanian oppression. The campaign in defense of Laszlo became an important element in the foreign policy of Hungary. The churches of Hungary, too, eventually broke their cautious silence and energetically took up the cause of Tokes.

The importance of Timisoara as the cradle of the revolution cannot be underestimated. The town had all the combustible elements for a mass uprising. Situated near the Hungarian and Yugoslav borders, the people of Timisoara had greater exposure to influences from the West than most citizens of Romania. The town had a history of uprising and revolt. Timisoara's university provided a strong army of enthusiastic foot soldiers for the anti-Ceausescu campaign. But above all, the relations between nationalities in Timisoara were traditionally respectful. Romanians were prepared to stand up and be counted when their Hungarian neighbor, Pastor Tokes, needed their support. Laszlo and the Hungarian community of Timisoara, for their part, engaged in acts of reconciliation rather than recrimination. Without this common front of Hungarians and Romanians, the Romanian revolution may well have been nipped in the bud.

Could a Romanian revolution have erupted without the witness of Laszlo Tokes? Yes, indeed. Laszlo's action was a major catalyst for the revolution. But his defiance coincided with the rapid internal decomposition of the Ceausescu system. In the autumn and winter of 1989, the collapse of Communism in Eastern Europe gained momentum. The sudden but peaceful revolutions in Czechoslovakia and East Germany swept away hard-line Communist regimes. In Poland, the Communists had already been forced to share power with the Catholic-backed Solidarity movement. The gradual evolution of neighboring Hungary into a multi-party democracy had reached an advanced stage. Ceausescu could expect no support from the reformist Gorbachev, who was himself presiding over a crumbling empire. Against this background of international isolation, the deterioration of the economy produced a volatile situation. Had Laszlo not provided the spark, another surely would have, or the dictator might have been removed from office by a coup of disgruntled military officers and reformist Communist politicians, such as the late General Milea and Ion Iliescu. The inflexible Ceausescu could not have indefinitely withstood the force of the East European Revolution that toppled one Communist dictator after another and shook the Soviet Union to its very foundations.

The End of the Ceausescus

The Ceausescus may not have been able to save their power, but they might have saved their skins were it not for their own excessive reliance on violence and their inflexible resistance to pressure for reform. Once their route to escape to a foreign country had been cut off, Nicolae and Elena were doomed. The only questions were how and when they would be dispatched to the hereafter.

The National Salvation Front government decided early on that its survival required the early death of the Ceausescus. The brief "trial" that preceded the executions was a bizarre judicial farce. The Ceausescus did not recognize the "court" and turned away their defense lawyer. The National Salvation Front government had already decided the two were to be executed and were giving the execution a veneer of legality. The charges against Ceausescu ranged from genocide (Article 356 of the Romanian Penal Code) to destroying buildings and state institutions and undermining the national economy (Articles 165 and 145). But there was little attempt to find out how far Ceausescu himself was guilty of each particular charge and how much he shared blame with others.

The political nature of the trial and the continuing fighting overshadowed the event and made a proper, fair trial impossible. But the swift execution—the firing squad opening fire with indecent haste—was generally applauded in Romania. The stirring sounds of Beethoven's "Ode to Joy" filled the airwaves immediately following the first broadcast of pictures of the Grand Conducator and his mistress lying dead in the dirt at their place of execution. In Nicolae's birthplace, villagers danced on the grave of his parents. Only abroad were strong reservations publicly expressed about the advisability of beginning a new era with such an execution. These were few and far between. Even before the Ceausescus had been captured, the future President of Czechoslovakia, Vaclav Havel, had called for just punishment but not the death penalty. "I ask all Romanian citizens," he said, "not to pay back violence with violence and cruelty with cruelty." In the case of Ceausescu and his wife, this advice was ignored.

Within Romania it was hard to find anyone—including Christians—who protested against the show trial or the executions. Eighty-four percent of the population were in favor of the executions, according to an opinion poll taken in mid-January. Laszlo was asked a few weeks after the revolution whether he thought the execution was justified. "In principle," he said, "I am against the death sentence. But I have learned that the present rule of Romania had to carry out this measure. The situation made it necessary to execute them." His thoughts were echoed by the Baptist pastor Paul Negrut. Speaking as a

Christian, he said, it was wrong to execute the couple. But speaking practically, the fighting would have continued a lot longer had they not been immediately executed. The fighting only died down once the Securitate units knew Ceausescu had been killed.

The execution was of enormous—though often unstated—significance. It set the tone of future developments. It was a bad omen for the primacy of the rule of law in Romania. The evil of the old regime extended beyond Nicolae and Elena. They left behind a brutal, autocratic system of government that was inherited by the National Salvation Front. The Front did introduce some noteworthy reforms. For example, almost immediately after the execution of the Ceausescus, the Front decreed the abolition of the death penalty. It also swiftly redirected agricultural produce from the export market to the hard-pressed domestic market. Rather grudgingly it permitted opposition parties and newspapers to operate. But the structures of the autocratic system, including the repressive domestic security apparatus, remained essentially unchanged. Many of those who had been in the forefront of the revolution on the streets of Timisoara, Bucharest and other cities were disappointed to discover after their "victory" that the Communists and fellow travelers who so faithfully served Ceausescu in the administration retained their posts.

The events that opened the eyes of the world to the ambiguous attitude toward democracy were the anti-Hungarian riots in Tirgu Mures and the calling in of the miners to clear students and other protesters from Bucharest's University Square. As the TV cameras rolled, the world could see that the new regime condoned mob violence if it was compatible with its own political interest.

A Second Revolution?

This brings us to a crucial question: Was the transfer of power a real revolution or a coup? Was the revolultion hijacked? Rumors abound that the key members of the National Salvation Front had some kind of plot worked out to remove Ceausescu from power and to place Romania on the course of reform Communism. The Front's swift consolidation of power showed a great degree of knowledge of the mechanisms of power. Its key members knew exactly what to do amid all the chaos. Some evidence suggests that the plot was to have taken place later in 1990 but was suddenly brought forward when the Timisoara demonstrations erupted and spread to other cities. The conspirators then moved in to take over the revolution, thus appearing to be the heroes of the revolution and the "saviors" of the nation.

Laszlo's view that Romania needs a second revolution to establish the rule of law and a genuine democratic system was echoed vehemently by most Transylvanian Hungarians. In Bucharest, the student protesters who spent two months in University Square defying Iliescu shared Laszlo's view. But the overwhelming majority of Romanians supported the National Salvation Front in the May elections. Now that the spasm of revolt has come to rest, Romanian political life has returned to traditional patterns of behavior.

The peoples of Romania do not have a history of democracy. The regions of Moldavia and Wallachia were under Turkish rule till the middle of the last century. Transylvania had a long history of constitutional government, but its constitution preserved the power and influence of the ruling elite. Prewar elections in Romania were rigged, and intimidation of political opponents was common. One Romanian observer of the political scene in the 1930s commented: "We have introduced universal suffrage, but with ballot-stuffing. We have centralized the administration of the country, but in the hands of parties. We have aped middle-class Europe in form, but at bottom we persist in the sycophantic habits of the past. In this way we have transformed political life into a hopeless turmoil." He could well have been referring to Romania in 1990. The fascism of the war years and the postwar Soviet-style Communism left no room for democracy. The demise of the Soviet system in Romania appears to be heralding the re-Balkanization of the country with all its corruption, inefficiency and brutality.

What about Romania's national minorities? How do they fit into the scheme of things in post-Ceausescu Romania? The outlook is not promising. The National Salvation Front government has suspended many of the more onerous anti-minority policies of the Ceausescu regime. Programs designed to discourage the survival of minorities and encourage assimilation are no longer vigorously executed. But the government shows a great reluctance to reverse the gains made by Ceausescu in weakening the position of the national minorities. Lip service is paid to respect for minority rights, but few concrete concessions are forthcoming from the government. Moreover, the authorities appear not to have the moral courage to defend the individual or collective rights of minorities under attack from extremist Romanian organizations.

With the collapse of Communism, Romanian nationalism is the most powerful political current in the country. The initial flush of good feeling of Romanians for Transylvania's Hungarians and the initial solidarity soon evaporated. The downplaying by the Front and other Romanian political bodies of the role of Laszlo Tokes and the Hungarians seems to have been deliberate. The anti-Hungarian riots in Tirgu Mures in March, 1990, further polarized the two nationalities. The reconcilation of Hungarians and Romanians that Laszlo and many others had been working for was undermined in a moment. Laszlo became the victim of a smear campaign for his defense of the Hungarian community.

The vast majority of Romanians share a passionate belief that the state ought to be entirely Romanian in ethnic character and that thriving national minorities with their own cultural and political institutions somehow threaten the unity of the state. The National Salvation Front is keenly aware of the strength of feeling among the ethnic Romanian majority on this issue and knows that by conscientiously defending minority rights, it would open the door to politically damaging charges of unpatriotism.

The position of most national minorities in post-Ceausescu Romania remains weak. Groups like the Slovaks and Ukrainians are small in number and have no powerful benefactors abroad. The Gypsies, though more significant numerically, have no tradition of defending their communities by political means. The once proud and prosperous German community has been decimated by officially approved emigration to West Germany. The outward flow of German refugees shows no signs of abating. The prospects of survival for the German community in Romania look bleak. The continuing flight of Germans reveals a signal lack of confidence in their future in Romania. The Germans were originally invited to Transylvania in the middle ages because of their Western skills and traditions. Those skills and traditions are needed now more than ever. The exodus of Germans from Romania is a bad omen for the country's prospects in the new Europe.

The Hungarians have a future in Transylvania. They are too numerous to emigrate en masse to Hungary. Moreover, the Hungarians tend to have a stronger attachment to the land and traditions of Transylvania than the Germans do. There will be significant Hungarian communities in the country for ages to come. The Hungarian spiritual and cultural revival so closely identified with Laszlo Tokes is extending the roots of the Hungarian community in Transylvanian soil. But whether or not the Hungarian community has a bright future depends mainly on the kind of society desired by the Romanian majority: a tolerant, pluralistic society in which ethnic differences can be constructively harmonized or an intolerant, uniform society in which the assimilation or exclusion of minorities is seen as a national priority.

The Future of the Church

For Christians, the restrictions on religion of the old regime have largely been lifted. One of the Front's first acts was to declare Christmas Day a public holiday—for the first time in 42 years. Religious prisoners were among prisoners of conscience set free in the revolution. The Eastern-rite Catholic Church was unbanned. The Lord's Army, a severely persecuted reform movement within the Orthodox Church, came out into the open. Summer camps for children, evangelistic meetings, the importation of Bibles and other Christian books, the broadcasting of religious services—all this, unthinkable under Ceausescu, could now take place again. Restrictions on seminary entry were lifted.

During 1990s Holy Week, *Jesus of Nazareth* was shown over five nights at peak viewing time on national TV. Foreign evangelists like Luis Palau were able to undertake unrestricted evangelistic visits. Leading Christians forced into exile, like the evangelical pastors Iosif Ton and Richard Wurmbrand, were able to return to the country. Christians were no longer afraid to attend church, to confess their faith openly and to welcome foreign Christians.

Churches could now organize themselves as they desired—the government could not stop them from choosing who they liked as leaders. Laszlo became bishop in one of the Reformed Church's two districts. The Baptist Church, too, was able to hold fresh elections. For the first time in many years, churches were not forced to "elect" someone the government had already chosen. For the first time, the Vatican was able to name new bishops for all the country's eleven dioceses.

Christians have to recognize they gained significantly from the revolution. Despite the upgrading of the government's controlling body, the Department of Religious Affairs, into a Ministry and the retention of many of its staff, the government withdrew from almost all of its day-to-day meddling in church affairs. Laszlo Tokes, as well as leading figures in other churches, including the Baptists, objected to the existence of the new Ministry. The old Department had only two sections before the revolution. When it became a Ministry it had six or eight sections, Paul Negrut declared in February. "I don't know why they need such a large staff to supervise churches that are supposed to be free." Many of the people from the old Department were in charge in the new Ministry. Laszlo put it like this: "We do not want any Ministry of Religious Affairs. We are autonomous church institutions and we do not need any paternalism from the state or interference in church matters."

Despite these misgivings about the Front's intentions, the revolution did largely take religious life out of the close control of the government. This was mainly brought about by the action of church leaders themselves, who no longer informed the ministry of their plans. They felt they should not have to seek government approval for their every action.

Politician or Pastor?

Was Laszlo's role political or religious? This question is still discussed today in Romanian church circles. Some Romanian Christians object that his motto "With God for the people" puts God in second place to the Transylvanian Hungarians. Suspicions linger about Laszlo's commitment to use Hungarian cultural traditions as a vehicle for preaching the Gospel to his flock. Romanian evangelicals are more inclined to use modern Western methods of public evangelism. The charge is also leveled that both before and after the revolution, Laszlo divided the Church and dragged it into the political arena, where it does not properly belong. Some feel Laszlo was more concerned with politics than with the saving of souls.

Laszlo does not deny an involvement in politics. But his continued role in public life is rooted in two of his fundamental beliefs. First, he believes God works through nations as well as individuals. The prophets of the Old Testament addressed nations, encouraging them to fulfill God's purpose. Jesus, too, ran into trouble for challenging the ecclesiastical and imperial power of His time. To retreat into the narrow realm of personal piety, in Laszlo's view, would be to abdicate responsibility for the world in which God placed mankind to live and work. Second, Laszlo respects the power of truth. One of Christianity's fundamental bases is truth. The Ceausescu regime denied truth with a system based on lies. Few others in Romania dared speak out. Laszlo felt obliged to do so. The lies must not go unchallenged. The system based on them would last forever until someone broke out of their slavery to them. Conscious of his prophetic role, Laszlo believed he had a divine obligation to speak out.

Many pastors within Laszlo's own Church felt that by antagonizing the regime unnecessarily and unproductively, he was making life harder for the whole Church. Some in the Church aimed to avoid conflict and tried to keep far away from the reaches of the regime. Laszlo could not do likewise, not for long anyway. Some pastors who tried their best to keep their parishes alive during the years of persecution and restriction sometimes found their lives getting harder as a result of Laszlo's dynamism. Laszlo was a divisive figure. Some people admired him—some openly, others in secret. Still more were secretly jealous of his growing authority and stature and his moral courage. A few considered his activity a distraction from what they perceived as the Church's main role: the dispensation of the sacraments and presiding over rights of passage. The rest—perhaps not very many—approved the government's moves to silence this turbulent young cleric.

Laszlo felt called for a ministry that went beyond the narrow bounds of routine pastoral work. He attacked restrictions on the Church—the lack of literature, limits on the number of seminarians, and state interference in internal Church life. But many of the issues he addressed —systematization, the assimilation of the Hungarian minority—were only indirectly religious. But in taking a stand on the side of truth, by refusing to compromise with an evil system and its unjust restrictions, he sought to live as a free man and show others the way to lose their fear. This was a moral choice.